For other books by Roderick Benns visit www.firesidepublishinghouse.com

"If we put our heads together, we don't have to accept a hodgepodge of programs. Welfare doesn't support anyone — it ensnares and entangles. It creates judgment. It is deeply problematic, wasteful, and expensive. This idea (of basic income) is attractive for all. Just give the money to the people living in poverty who will know what to do with it."

The Honourable Hugh Segal

A Note to the Reader

As this book demonstrates, I've managed to talk to a lot of people about basic income over the last two years, a fact for which I am very grateful. This book contains virtually all of the writing I have ever done on basic income, including Q&A sessions that were conducted.

By listening and writing about the needs of community leaders such as mayors and councillors from municipalities across Canada, it gave me an idea of some of the challenges that exist at the local level. By listening to senators, ministers, and members of parliament, I was able to understand some of the policy challenges and opportunities about basic income and inequality.

I was also fortunate to speak with so many academics, many who have spent decades studying basic income, inequality, and the marginalizing effects of poverty.

Finally, the people who had experienced poverty firsthand were instrumental in opening my eyes to what a basic income policy might have meant for them, either when they were younger or even now.

It has been my pleasure to listen to the views of so many people because it has helped immeasurably to clarify my own beliefs about this vital social policy.

For instance, in Canada, the type of basic income that has the most support is a negative income tax model – and I've come to accept this vision. In this model, a basic income would be universally available to anyone who needs it when their income drops below a certain threshold. This is certainly a more affordable option than the demogrant model where everyone receives the same basic income regardless of their own net worth or annual wage.

I now believe that a basic income set at $18,000 to $20,000 per year is most reasonable. Let's say it was set at $18,000. If someone earns

$13,000 from working, then a basic income guarantee would kick in with $5,000, spread out in equal monthly payments over 12 months.

Such a basic income must be nimble enough and responsive enough to help with the realities of precarious work. It should be accompanied by a national Pharmacare program and a national childcare program. Housing supports should also be available since not enough affordable housing exists right now, especially in Canada's three key metropolitan areas.

To pay for and organize such a basic income, I believe we should eliminate all of the welfare systems across Canada, which have poorly served people living in poverty. In fact, such programs have further embedded poverty within our communities.

I also believe we should be eliminating Employment Insurance (EI), given its failed mandate. At one time it was meant to be a springboard for people in between jobs. Increasingly stringent eligibility requirements and vastly reduced payouts have made it nothing more than a government cash cow and a mockery of its original intent.

I believe a basic income will strengthen social capital formation and lead to greater civic engagement. I believe a basic income will lead to significantly better health outcomes and that population health is a primary reason for advocating for such a policy.

Under a basic income I believe that some people will indeed stop working, but that they will be a minority. If the program is set up correctly with strong work incentives, people will continue to want to add to what is only a 'basic' income, as the name suggests.

Partly because contract and temporary work is so prevalent now, I believe we need to expand our definition of work. Our definition of work must change to include not just wage labour but the work we do each day in caring for children, older family members, volunteering, and participating in civic life.

A Pilot in Canada's Largest Province

As I write this in early October of 2016, a basic income pilot is about to be announced in detail by the Province of Ontario. This is a big deal, with worldwide ramifications within the basic income movement. Ontario is Canada's second largest province in area, covering more than one million square kilometres — an area larger than France and Spain combined. It is the largest province by population in Canada, with more than 13.5 million people. This single province generates 37 percent of the national GDP.

So it is a political region with clout that is larger than many nations, embedded inside a G7 country that at one time was a leader in social policy development. Creating a basic income for its citizens could propel Canada to the forefront in social policy once again.

Expertise

Most of the people inside this book who I interviewed have more knowledge, expertise, and experience in thinking about basic income policy than me. I thank them for their time and energy for this cause. I would also like to acknowledge my wife, Joli Scheidler-Benns, for her vital role in setting up the Canadian mayors' survey on basic income. Appreciation is also extended to my expert co-writers on a handful of these articles, too, and I thank them for allowing their words to appear in this book format as well as on my news site, *Leaders and Legacies*.

It is my hope this book will add to the dialogue on inequality and provide further proof that the time for a basic income is now.

Roderick Benns

A basic income guarantee should be Canada's next great social program

Jan 12, 2015

By Roderick Benns

We have built something exceptional here in Canada, despite coming of age beside the world's most powerful country. What we have built, though, is in danger of collapse because of poverty -- and that includes the well-being of our middle and upper class.

There is no doubt that John A. Macdonald's vision, coupled with our geo-political reality, endowed us with a unique heritage. What Macdonald also did was to pave the way for others to build on the Canadian dream.

And they have.

Successive leaders after Macdonald built or expanded tremendous social programs (Richard Bennett, William Lyon Mackenzie King, Saskatchewan's Tommy Douglas, Lester Pearson, Pierre Trudeau, and more) while others have demonstrated that opening our borders to vibrant free markets can co-exist alongside programs we have built for the social good (Brian Mulroney). Through the years, we have become a G-7 nation and one of the wealthiest societies in the world.

While the United States rejected the vision of a caring nation state — doing so in favour of an overall individual responsibility for personal welfare — the twisted result has been a form of social imprisonment for many of its own citizens. There is a vast gap between the rich and the poor; low minimum wages threaten even the working class; a lack of Medicare for millions has ensured American citizens are less 'free' than their history promised.

Canada is in no position to become complacent. The gap between the rich and the poor here is also widening, and at a startling rate. Addressing inequality is our greatest challenge, but it should not be seen as a lament of the left wing. Societies that do not strive for equality are failed societies.

Harvard philosopher T. M. Scanlon notes there are four reasons for addressing inequality. First, there is the obvious moral reason — but there are also practical ones.

"Income inequality means that some children will...find it harder to access the first small steps to larger opportunities, such as a loan to start a business or pay for an advanced degree," Scanlon writes.

He also notes that workers, as part of a cooperative effort to create a national income, have an honest claim to "a fair share of what they have helped to produce."

(By virtue of good national policy, Canada has avoided Scanlon's fourth reason for addressing inequality -- namely, that politicians who depend on large contributions for their campaigns will be more responsive to the interests of the rich. In Canada, a person can only give up to $1,200 each year, in total, to each registered political party. Corporations and trade unions may not make contributions at all.)

The $20,000 Solution

There is a movement that has been gaining steam in Canada to create a basic income guarantee as Canada's next key social program. In some ways, it's incredibly simple. No man or woman in Canada would ever fall below a $20,000 annual income threshold.

In other words, if you worked part time while putting yourself through school and earned $12,000 a year, then the basic income guarantee program would kick in with $8,000 at tax time.

The biggest elephant in the room is the fear that a large cross-section of people will simply stop working. But there is ample evidence to suggest this simply won't happen. In Dauphin, Manitoba, from 1974 to 1979, the federal and provincial governments of Canada provided money to every person and family in Dauphin who were living below the poverty line. The program was called Mincome (minimum income) and it affected the lives of about 1,000 families who received monthly cheques as part of the experiment. For a family of five, payments equalled about $18,000 a year in today's dollars.

Finding Meaning in Our Lives

Many years later, Dr. Evelyn Forget, a professor in the Department of Community Health Sciences at the University of Manitoba, took a second look at the results. She found there was only a slight decline in work – and that was mostly among mothers, who made the choice to stay home with their children longer. She also found that teenagers decided to stay in school longer, that hospital visits declined, and that mental health visits were also reduced.

The Mincome project was quietly pre-empted by a change in government at the provincial level, and a nervous economic situation at the federal level, as a world oil crisis played out. But what it showed us is what many social scientists have long believed – that people are hardwired to find meaning in their lives. When one is overly preoccupied with the next meal or paying the rent on time, it leaves little room for daring to dream about other opportunities. It's difficult to go back to school to better oneself, to innovate new ideas, or simply to do a good, attentive job of raising a family. Mincome showed that if we take the worry of poverty off people's shoulders, there's a much better chance to create a richer, more meaningful society for everyone.

When a Senate committee made rough calculations six years ago, they found it would cost about $20 billion to implement such a basic income program. It's undoubtedly a lot of money, and yet not prohibitive for one of the world's wealthiest nations. Contrast this with a 2008 study, estimating that $72 billion to $86 billion as the cost of health care, criminal justice and lost productivity, all associated with the crippling effects of poverty. In other words, we would actually be saving money to implement a basic income guarantee.

As for paying for such a program, it's quite possible the following massive programs could eventually be dismantled:

- the entire welfare system
- disability support
- employment insurance

These three enormous programs could be made obsolete by a basic income guarantee. Such a new approach would be simpler, it would save money, and it would make us healthier, safer, and save lives.

A Program for the Left and Right

Those who lean left on the political spectrum can appreciate the obvious goal of ending poverty for all. Even those on the far right hand side of political opinion, who may only wish to talk about economic models, should appreciate a more simplified tax code, far less bureaucracy, and a chance for all Canadians to have more money to spend in our economy.

A recent poll conducted by the Pierre Elliott Trudeau Foundation indicates slight majority support for a basic income plan for Canadians. Let us build on this support with a sense of urgency. *Leaders and Legacies* calls for the federal government, in cooperation with the provinces and municipalities, to coordinate a handful of pilot projects across Canada that properly mirrors the complexity of Canadian society. A long-term study will yield new data on this important issue.

Unlike our southern neighbour, Canada began as an egalitarian nation of modest means. We didn't have a dominant upper class -- we just had people working together in common cause. Today, nearly 150 years later, we can ensure that we continue to nation build and be more egalitarian again. This time, though, we can do so from a position of collective strength, not collective struggle, given the wealth and opportunity we have built together.

The toleration of poverty is a continuing blight on our national legacy, in a country where we should have a democratic right to equity. Canada has been blessed with a legacy of great leaders. It will be great leadership again – at national, provincial, and community levels – that creates an equitable Canadian society of opportunity for all.

We can't eliminate child poverty if the parents are poor: Green Party leader Elizabeth May

January 12, 2015

By Roderick Benns

Canada's three main parties pledged in 1989 to end child poverty before the year 2000, a failed promise that today many are lamenting. But federal Green Party leader Elizabeth May says the answer is not to focus on children, but poor people overall.

"We can't eliminate child poverty if the parents are poor."

Among the various ways of ensuring a basic income guarantee, the Green Party of Canada believes the best policy is a negative income tax, or Guaranteed Livable Income. In an interview with *Leaders and Legacies*, May points out the Green Party platform calls for this approach, which could "eliminate poverty and allow social services to concentrate on problems of mental health and addiction."

The Green platform would provide a regular payment to every Canadian without regard to a needs test, with the level of the payment "regionally set at a level above poverty, but at a bare subsistence level to encourage additional income generation."

"We believe that we'll need to have negotiations, federally and provincially, and that many other programs can then be wrapped up. We'll no longer need all the various types of welfare programs" that all provinces have in varying degrees, she says.

May says her party believes that no one should be taxed on income until they (as an individual) earn more than $20,000. As for paying for such a program, May says the Green platform declares that eliminating poverty while supporting healthy communities "will pay

11

for itself in reduced health care costs, as poverty is the single largest determinant of ill health."

A reduction in crime would also see great savings, according to the Green's policy planks. May believes the best strategy for seeing some form of guaranteed livable income is for more public awareness by taking the time to have conversations across the country.

It's become too acceptable to shrug it off. It will be more supported if people found out why it works and why it makes sense for the economy."

May says she is "grateful" that retired Conservative Senator Hugh Segal is talking about this, which helps illustrate that a guaranteed income is not just policy for the 'left.'

"I think it's important for it to be considered good policy across the country," says May, regardless of political affiliation.

When May reflects on the Green's poverty policy seminar in 2007, she recalls connecting with some of the original researchers who worked on the Dauphin, Manitoba guaranteed annual income experiment.

In Dauphin, from 1974 to 1979, the federal and provincial governments provided money to every person and family in Dauphin who were below the poverty line. For a family of five, payments equalled about $18,000 a year in today's dollars.

Years later, Evelyn Forget, a professor in the Department of Community Health Sciences at the University of Manitoba, took a second look at those results. She found there was only a slight decline in work – mostly among mothers, who made the choice to stay home with their children longer. She also found that young people chose to stay in school longer.

"It was clear that people seized the opportunity to go back to school and improve their skills," says May of the research. "The evidence was quite reassuring," and the fear that people "would just become permanently unemployed" ended up being unfounded.

"It just didn't happen. People saw it as an opportunity to improve their education and get ahead. It wasn't shame-based -- it was simply a very good approach to improving the health of a society," says May.

May says any approach that raises awareness on a consistent basis should be welcome. That could be pilot projects, conversations in parliament, and conversations through the media.

"I think this is something that requires federal-provincial collaboration. So many of the programs that put Band-Aids on poverty cost this nation a lot at both levels. We'd be much better off to have a national strategy."

Researcher says Basic Income Guarantee could be gradually introduced into Canadian life

January 15, 2015

By Roderick Benns

It was called a landmark social experiment in its time. From 1974 to 1979, the federal and provincial governments of Canada provided money to every person and family in Dauphin who were living below the poverty line.

It was researcher Evelyn Forget who revived interest in this experiment, after she spent time looking at the effects of what they called 'Mincome' (minimum income) and how it affected the lives of about 1,000 families.

Forget dug up the records from the period and found there were some significant benefits in the education and health sectors, such as an 8.5 percent drop in hospital visits, fewer emergency room visits, and less recorded incidents of domestic abuse. As well, less people sought treatment for mental health issues and more high school students continued on to finish Grade 12 to graduate.

Forget is an economist, professor in the Department of Community Health Sciences at the University of Manitoba, and Academic Director of the Manitoba Research Data Centre. In a recent interview with *Leaders and Legacies*, she says everything she has read and studied has led her to the conclusion that Canada would benefit from a basic income guarantee.

"I think removing some of the gaps and roadblocks in the current system and empowering people to make their own decisions is a very positive thing. Eliminating the waste of having very well trained social workers spending all their time trying to access basic income support for their clients, rather than doing something more positive can only be beneficial," she says.

Forget notes that if the federal government wanted to revive interest in doing some pilot projects across Canada on this issue, there would need to be good federal-provincial cooperation.

"The real problem in Canada is that income support is a provincial responsibility," says Forget. "If a basic income guarantee is offered federally, it needs to be made consistent with existing provincial income support schemes, unless we imagine that we can get all premiers and the feds to come to an agreement."

She says one possibility might be to retain existing schemes, and use the basic income guarantee as a 'top-up' in a way similar to that of the Child Tax Benefit.

"Over time, the transfers from the federal government used to support provincial schemes could be frozen...and the basic income guarantee enhanced — a very gradual replacement of existing schemes with the new program."

Forget says this would also buy time to ensure that no group is disadvantaged by the basic income guarantee, such as people with disabilities.

"In general, I like the gradual approach and I think it is more consistent with Canadian policy-making than a wholesale replacement of one system by another."

As for what towns, cities, or areas should be a part of a pilot project, Forget says there is much to consider for balance. She says the following things would need to be taken into account:

- A site or sites should be chosen that are broadly representative of Canada in terms of age, structure, and demography – not an old population or a young population, but representative.
- There should be an urban site and a small town site.
- The urban site should have a significant immigrant population
- Since First Nations people (both on and off reserve) are significantly more likely to be low income, then this should also be a consideration.
- A site should be chosen that has a representative job market — not purely resource-based or seasonal, but one with a balanced economy.

Setting up a program like a basic income guarantee is complex, Forget says, because there are a number of choices, all with implications "for costs as well as outcomes."

"There is a very good reason to tie the income to individuals, because it empowers all members of a family. However, our current tax and transfer system is based on family income."

She says in order to be consistent, Canada and the provinces would either have to make many changes in the current system or make a basic income guarantee dependent on family income.

Canadian senator says basic income must go mainstream

January 20, 2015

By Roderick Benns

One of the most outspoken Canadian politicians on inequality says it's time to get 10 percent of Canadians taking action to support a basic income guarantee.

Senator Art Eggleton says that inequality is pulling Canada down in too many ways. To make an impact, Eggleton tells *Leaders and Legacies* that "political will needs to be created."

He points out something that Malcolm Gladwell popularized — that when just 10 percent of the population holds an unshakable belief and are willing to take action to support it, that same belief will soon be adopted by the majority of society.

"So let's just get 10 percent of us really moving in this direction to make the change we desperately need," Eggleton says.

The senator says that for a rich nation, "we have far too many people living in poverty."

"Morally, it's wrong. We shouldn't be having people living without enough food, or clothing, or decent shelter. But it also costs us a fortune," he notes.

Eggleton says the study he most frequently cites was the one produced by economists for the Ontario Association of Food Banks, who found that poverty costs the government about $30 billion a year. Other organizations peg that closer to a minimum of $72 billion annually. Much of this is connected to health care costs, he says, since being poor too often means poor health.

"And that $30 billion doesn't even include the bureaucracy of the welfare system and the thousands of pages of rules and regulations that trap people in poverty," Eggleton says passionately. "We can do far better."

He acknowledges that it will take a while to get there, but that ultimately a basic income guarantee would be more efficient and effective. "If people have the means, they will be able to contribute better to the economy because they will then spend more into the economy."

Eggleton says ordinary Canadians must make sure politicians move inequality to the front burners, to "get it on their agenda."

A recent poll conducted by the Pierre Elliott Trudeau Foundation indicates slight majority support for a basic income plan for Canadians, but the senator emphasizes taking action. "Invite politicians to your community to talk. Write to them. Get in front of them — this is very helpful."

Eggleton says if politicians don't feel that it connects or matters for their constituents, "then they look at other issues."

"Politicians are so tied up in the day-to-day and not the long term."

The senator says that when the election campaigns come around, pollsters ask people what their key issues are, and poverty is not generally on the table. For one reason, he says, the people in poverty likely aren't answering many phones for the pollsters. "So it's up to all of us to make this issue matter -- and it's something that really affects all of us, too."

Senator Art Eggleton presses Trudeau to adopt basic income guarantee if Liberals win

Jan 21 2015

By Roderick Benns

It's not something federal Liberal leader Justin Trudeau will be allowed to forget, if Senator Art Eggleton has his way.

Early in 2014, at a Liberal policy convention, two resolutions were made and accepted by delegates that steer the Liberal Party of Canada toward a basic income guarantee for working-age Canadians.

Eggleton says this is significant, and he has been talking it up wherever he goes.

"I take some delight in what happened at the Liberal convention in the spring," he tells *Leaders and Legacies*. "And when I recently saw Justin I reminded him of that — and I told him he should promise" that Liberals will make this a reality.

Eggleton refers to resolution number 97 (*Basic Income Supplement: Testing a Dignified Approach to Income Security for Working-age Canadians*) and resolution number 100 (*Creating a Basic Annual Income to be Designed and Implemented for a Fair Economy*), both of which were adopted by federal Liberal delegates.

He says Trudeau "listened and recognized what I was talking about" but was non-committal in his face-to-face meeting with the senator.

"But I've been planting the seed with others members of his caucus as well," laughs Eggleton.

One thing the Liberal senator says is important to kick-start the program is to create a pilot project. The example of Mincome, in Dauphin, Manitoba, is now dated and a fresh approach to a pilot project would be of great value for researchers and policy analysts.

"In order to build political will we need a contemporary pilot project, and I'm hopeful that's what we can do."

Eggleton says a pilot project is the best way to dispel concerns that people will give up working if their basic needs are met. A basic income guarantee, he says, "isn't the good life, it's the basics."

"The vast majority of people want to do more than that. We use up enormous resources of thought examining whether or not people will stop working if we ensure they aren't in poverty. This just isn't true. Our worry that people are going to laze around and not get jobs is ludicrous."

As the Mincome experiment from the 1970s showed, says the senator, is that the small percentage of people who did stop working were mothers who wanted to stay home with their young children for a bit longer or youth who wanted to finish school.

"I'd say both of those are good things."

Eggleton – as a four-term Toronto mayor — was recently appointed by Mayor John Tory to head a task force charged with examining the governance of Toronto's social housing corporation. With regard to affordable housing, Eggleton believes that social housing will still be around, even with a basic income guarantee.

"We do need people who work at various levels, at various wages, in a mixed economy. But Toronto is expensive. Some people will have a difficult time in finding suitable housing. Commutes are expensive in time and money," the senator says.

"We will always need housing suitable for different income levels. Childhood education is also a key thing. A basic income is just basic - - it can't be everything." But, says the senator, it's a great start.

Eggleton says that he hopes a basic income guarantee proposal will be firmly adopted "by one or more parties" that are firmly committed to doing a pilot project.

Important to extend discussion of basic income guarantee to a variety of political leaders, says university dean

February 4, 2015

Roderick Benns recently interviewed Dr. James Mulvale, dean of the Faculty of Social Work at the University of Manitoba, about a basic income guarantee. Dr. Mulvale is one of the guest speakers at the University of Manitoba's February symposium, 'A Basic Income for Canada and Manitoba: Why Not?'

Benns: *Do you believe that a leaner bureaucracy is possible — including the eventual elimination of disability, welfare, and employment insurance with a basic income guarantee?*

Mulvale: In principle, Basic Income would be simpler to administer than our current complicated, means-and-needs-tested array of income assistance programs (especially 'last resort' programs such as social assistance at the provincial level). We currently have income-tested, Basic-income-like payments determined through our income tax returns (Guaranteed Income Supplement for seniors, GST/PST rebate, Working Income Tax Benefit, and the Canada Child Tax Benefit).

I think that we have to evolve in a step by step fashion towards a more comprehensive and generous guaranteed income 'architecture' that is a federal-provincial partnership. It may be possible, over time, to reduce and perhaps eventually eliminate our reliance on disability and unemployment benefits. But in getting from here to there, we must not leave people worse off in the meantime. And we also must have flexible benefit programs that can recognize special needs — for example the extra income support that persons with disabilities might need for assistive devices, accessible transportation, and so on.

An advantage of Basic Income is that it can move us away from intrusive and stigmatizing 'welfare policing.' At the same time, better income support does not mean that we can eliminate necessary services for those who need social support -- such as child and family programs, mental health and addiction services and social housing programs.

Benns: *From your perspective and background, what makes a basic income guarantee attractive as a policy option?*

Mulvale: Its relative simplicity and efficiency, as already mentioned. Its recognition of human freedom and the right to make individual life choices. Its potential to move us away from economic growth and the creation of paid jobs as the primary policy option that is supposed to ensure economic security for all. This is a pre-requisite if we are to move towards a 'steady state' and an ecologically sustainable economy.

Benns: *Why are most politicians so reticent to touch this issue and how can we shift perspectives?*

Mulvale: I think that politicians of a variety of political stripes are giving serious thought to the basic income approach. The federal Green Party under Elizabeth May, former Conservative Senator Hugh Segal, Liberal Senator Art Eggleton, Prince Edward Island Liberal Premier Robert Ghiz, the federal Liberal Party – through two policy resolutions at its most recent convention – and the Progressive Conservative Leader of the Opposition in Manitoba.

There is also the Quebec Minister of Social Solidarity, François Blais, who sees Basic Income as at least a longer-term goal. The basic income approach has also been supported by the Conference Board of Canada in some of its publications. It seems to me that we must foster and extend these discussions in various political circles and with various political leaders.

McGill fellow believes a basic income needs other targeted social programs

February 5, 2015

Roderick Benns recently interviewed Jurgen De Wispelaere, a fellow at the Institute for Health and Social Policy at McGill University, Montreal, about a basic income guarantee. De Wispelaere is a founding editor of the journal Basic Income Studies, co-editor of three books, and author of dozens of peer-reviewed articles.

Benns: *In what way can Canada draw from Nordic nations' experiences when it comes to inequality? Out of Norway, Sweden, Denmark, and Finland, what nation is on the right track these days when it comes to helpful social policy?*

De Wispelaere: I am not an expert on Scandinavian social democratic policy regimes, but a few small points in response. The Nordic countries are very different from Canada and we have to be careful about learning lessons from other countries, or rather about thinking that we can apply models across very easily. In addition, the Nordic countries differ quite a lot internally as well, and have evolved quite differently in the last 10 years, so it all depends what aspect of social policy you are interested in. In terms of Basic Income Guarantee, the country to watch out for is Finland, where the discussion is most developed and active.

Benns: *In what way would you try to convince someone who is on the conservative (right) side of politics about the merits of a basic income guarantee?*

De Wispelaere: This is an interesting one. It's often said that Basic Income Guarantee is a great policy because it has supporters across the political spectrum, but I would like to add a note of caution to that claim. Basic Income Guarantee, at the most general level, obscures so that we often end up talking about proposals that are quite different at the level of detailed design. Unsurprisingly, progressives and conservatives propose very different models in terms of costing or the funding source, implementation modalities, focus on individual or household-based, and most controversially which programs can be abolished once we institute a Basic Income.

This disagreement is substantial, so the key question for Basic Income advocates is whether we go with a strategy of agreeing on the basics and working out the details as we go along, or whether instead we want to be very clear about our 'red lines' and if need be build a progressive coalition and leave the conservatives outside. Pragmatic politics is one thing, but too much compromise might eat into the very reasons we want the policy in the first place. Hard choices!

Benns: *Do you believe that a leaner bureaucracy is possible – including the eventual elimination of disability, welfare, and employment insurance with a basic income guarantee?*

De Wispelaere: In a sense my response here continues on the previous point. The one argument that is often put forward to the conservative side is the so-called administrative savings argument, but this in my view is very much a red herring. There is no doubt that Basic Income is easier to administer than its selective counterparts, but what produces savings is not the extra implementation of a Basic Income but rather whether it replaces other policies. And here lies the rub: as said before, for progressives Basic Income will always be complemented with a wide range of targeted social programs so the actual administrative machinery is not being reduced as is sometimes suggested.

Basic Income would never be able to fully replace disability assistance, welfare or unemployment insurance as you suggest – not for progressives at least. The sort of program that would really amount to a lot of savings has been proposed by some Conservatives (for instance by the controversial US social commentator Charles Murray), but is entirely unpalatable outside these circles.

One more point on administration. The anti-bureaucracy perspective of many Basic Income advocates actually poses an interesting political problem: social history teaches us that once a policy becomes implemented, its administration constitutes one important interest group that protects the policy against political backlash; the 'lean bureaucracy' argument may well be a recipe for reduced stability over time for Basic Income.

A basic income guarantee would deal directly with poverty, says economics professor

February 5, 2015

Roderick Benns recently interviewed Dr. Wayne Simpson, a Professor in the Department of Economics at the University of Manitoba, about a basic income guarantee. Dr. Simpson is a graduate of the University of Saskatchewan and the London School of Economics. He is one of the guest speakers at the University of Manitoba's February symposium, 'A Basic Income for Canada and Manitoba: Why Not?'

Benns: *Do you believe that a leaner bureaucracy is possible – including the eventual elimination of disability, welfare, and employment insurance with a basic income guarantee?*

Simpson: A leaner bureaucracy might occur because a basic income guarantee — I prefer guaranteed annual income — is delivered through the existing tax system along the lines of the Child Tax Benefit and other refundable tax credits. But the replacement of welfare, a provincial responsibility, with a guaranteed annual income is a provincial matter and replacement of Employment Insurance treats EI solely as an income maintenance program rather than a wage insurance program, which it is partly. So it is hard to say how such programs would be impacted by a guaranteed annual income at the federal level.

Benns: *From your perspective and background, what makes a basic income guarantee attractive as a policy option?*

Simpson: It deals directly with the problem of poverty and low incomes and effectively targets the low income population, which many current income support programs do not. Welfare does this, but is inadequate and delivered ineffectively outside the tax system.

Benns: *How would you approach this debate with someone on the 'right' side of the political spectrum? What is the best approach in talking with conservative-minded people about this issue in terms of getting them to see the policy's attractiveness?*

Simpson: The argument has always been that the problem of poverty should be attacked directly by a guaranteed annual income rather than indirectly and frequently by a series of programs that are poorly targeted to the poor. In particular, we should not fool around with the market system – for example, minimum wage legislation – to reduce poverty.

Benns: *Why are most politicians so reticent to touch this issue and how can we shift perspectives?*

Simpson: The GAI was seriously considered in the 1970s but other events (stagflation and budget deficits) drove it off the stage. It is a bold move that is not a particularly strong vote-getter, since the poor have a weak voting record. The focus on the middle class (however defined) reflects their influence as voters and I don't see them citing poverty and a guaranteed annual income as important issues.

Waterloo group works to make basic income guarantee part of the conversation

February 10, 2015

By Roderick Benns

John Green had careers in both information technology and publishing before health reasons forced him to quit his work. In a G7 nation of spectacular wealth, the Waterloo resident suddenly found himself on disability benefits and living well below the poverty line.

While Canada has regularly been ranked one of the top 10 places to lives in the world for 21 consecutive years by both the United Nations and the Economist Intelligence Unit, there is another, more troubling story that continues to unfold – the creeping distance between those who have and those who have not.

For people like Green, who always had an interest in inequality as a policy issue, it was now an issue that suddenly hit home. A year ago, Green mobilized an advocacy group called Basic Income Waterloo Region. Serving as coordinator of the organization, Green points out that it' s modelled after the Basic Income Canada Network, for which he also volunteers in a communications capacity.

In general, a basic income guarantee would ensure that no one in Canada would ever fall below the poverty line. The government would 'top up' anyone who didn't meet this threshold, which is often pegged at $20,000 per year.

Green's group works to build public support in Waterloo Region for a basic income guarantee policy (also called guaranteed annual income) at a grassroots level. His group works to engage with politicians in as many electoral districts as possible. He notes the regional groups, like Waterloo's, are all generally sympathetic to

BICN's goals and messaging but are not controlled by the national group in any way, and nor do they speak for the national group.

Green says there is "general dissatisfaction with current government income-support programs and approaches to addressing poverty."

"In the past year or so, I have met with people from many agencies and groups who work with people living in poverty, and I have been heartened by their generally positive responses to the idea of a basic income guarantee," says Green.

When asked if a basic income guarantee would be likely to replace existing social programs, Green acknowledges some people get nervous about this idea. He knows that some people would worry they might be worse off than before, if a basic income guarantee were to replace other forms of social benefits.

"My opinion is that many existing income-support programs — including welfare, Old Age Security, the GST rebate, the Canada Child Tax Benefit and many other tax credits — could safely be replaced with a well-designed basic income guarantee."

Green says that the livable benefit level his group advocates for is roughly $20,000 per adult and $6000 per child. This "is higher than any existing income support program in Canada" that is currently paid.

"So recipients of existing programs would be better off under this kind of basic income guarantee."

Green says they would be better off in two ways. First, the amount of income received would be greater than what they currently receive, and secondly "there would be far fewer, if any, rules or conditions to meet in order to qualify."

This would also reduce bureaucracy considerably. One possible exception, he notes, is Employment Insurance, where the maximum benefit is slightly higher, but yet not everyone receives the maximum.

"And many unemployed people don't qualify for EI benefits at all."

Green says it would be good to see some statistics on typical EI benefits received before forming any strong opinions about replacing EI. Other existing programs could have their income-support component replaced with the basic income guarantee, he says, but yet continue to provide specialized supports unique to each person's needs.

"For example, disability programs could continue to provide the extra supports needed by people with disabilities, including extra financial support to cover expensive medications or assistive devices, while the basic income guarantee would provide income for regular living expenses."

Green says the system would still need to be in place to help out with non-financial supports, such as affordable housing, employment supports, assistance in filing income tax returns, and drug, dental and vision coverage.

For Basic Income Waterloo Region, Green says they will continue to focus on networking and building alliances with anti-poverty groups and agencies in the region, "hoping that they will include basic income in the conversation when they engage with local politicians."

Welfare must go and should be replaced by a basic income: Basic Income Canada chair

Feb 11, 2015

Roderick Benns recently interviewed Sheila Regehr, chair of the Basic Income Canada Network, about a basic income guarantee for Canadians.

Benns: *Based on what we've learned in Dauphin, Manitoba and in some international lessons, if the federal government were to try a basic income guarantee experiment again — perhaps in a few centres in Canada — what should they consider about their site choices?*

Regehr: The most important part of this question is 'what we've learned.' We've learned that a basic income can actually support labour force participation rather than discourage it as some fear. Thanks to Dr. Evelyn Forget's recent work on the Dauphin site, and to other international programs, we also know that a basic income can generate wide societal benefits for the community, such as better health, increased education and fewer accidents and injuries.

Basic Income Canada Network doesn't have a formal position on the need for new pilots. Pilots may be important to getting politicians on board. In the case of Prince Edward Island, there is an active basic income group and political leaders seem to be very interested, so that could lead to good things. Some people are wary that pilots can also be used as a stalling tactic. If there are to be pilots, what is most important is that we not just retest old assumptions but rather build on what we've learned. Because Canada already has forms of basic income for seniors and children, we can learn from those experiences as well.

Benns: *Broadly, in what way would you like to see this program set up in Canada? And, what might be eliminated to make it happen, such as welfare?*

Regehr: Basic Income Canada Network is open to exploring a range of possible options. Canada has experience with universal demogrant and negative income tax delivery methods, and a combination of the two. Seniors and children's benefits both have a very broad-based benefit and elements geared to support those with lower incomes. There are several refundable tax credits that also support those with limited resources. Contrary to this pattern, welfare is rather a relic of earlier times that does not suit the 21st century. It is stigmatizing, and often punitive and harmful, so it is certainly the one program that must be effectively replaced. For others, it depends on the extent to which Canadians want significant overhaul or an option that builds around what already works.

Benns: *There are even Conservative voices on the side of this issue. Why is that?*

Regehr: Polls and research show that a basic income has broad appeal that does not fit neatly into traditional political categories. Many people feel that government should not interfere too much with people's daily lives and that would include welfare bureaucracies. Some see the economic logic of putting money directly into the hands of people who need it as a way of making a free market more of a reality.

A hard look at public finances shows how costly poverty is to a society so there is a strong business case for a basic income. Many people with a more conservative perspective have great concern for others who are less advantaged and recognize that old methods aren't working. Across the political spectrum there is growing concern about the impact of extreme income inequalities and a precarious labour market.

Benns: *More than half of Canadians seem to want this program, when you look at opinion polls. How can this broad support actually turn into meaningful political support to make it happen?*

Regehr: From BICN's perspective, a key ingredient to making a basic income a reality is to generate as much informed public conversation as possible, and there are many ways to do that, including in an election year by attending candidates meetings and asking questions. There is rarely one route to policy change and the more places and ways that basic income is talked about the higher it will climb on the public agenda. There are signals that political leaders are listening so we need to keep the volume turned up.

Benns: *Medicare started in Canada when one province – Saskatchewan — decided to do things differently. Does this suggest we could see provincial leadership on this issue as likely we are to see federal? Are there any provinces, to your knowledge, that are amenable to these ideas?*

Regehr: Yes, provincial leadership is a possibility. One way would be to go it alone. It might not be easy but John Stapleton has put forward a proposal showing that Ontario could do it. As mentioned before, there seems to be political interest in Prince Edward Island. There are other ways that provinces, territories and municipalities (especially large ones like Toronto, where the neighbourhood effects of income polarization are a huge challenge) can show leadership. In fact many have already done so, for example by creating poverty reduction strategies.

It is in their interests to try to get the federal government on board with a basic income because they bear the responsibility and costs of health and other services that patch up the consequences of growing inequality and insecurity. Collectively, these other orders of government could have a powerful influence.

Basic income guarantee group in Kingston tackles issue one kitchen table at a time

March 2, 2015

Roderick Benns recently interviewed Toni Pickard, coordinator of Kingston Action Group, which supports a basic income guarantee for Canadians.

Benns: *How long has the Kingston Action Group for Basic Income Guarantee been around, and are there other social issues which you advocate for?*

Pickard: In November of 2013, the co-founder of the group and I each invited a few people to an informal meeting with Rob Rainer to talk about his fledgling Basic Income Guarantee (BIG) Push campaign for basic income. The next month most of us reconvened to work in earnest to support his campaign. A core group of seven has been working steadily since then. Others have come and gone and we now have about 13 members. The name Kingston Action Group for BIG has evolved over time.

We've always focused uniquely on basic income and are too busy with that to think about working on other important issues that we support in spirit. We have two main goals: to spread awareness and generate discussion and support with the aim of creating a grassroots movement for basic income; and to secure political support for the BIG concept.

Benns: *What have you noticed happening in the Kingston Region that gives you hope about a basic income guarantee?*

Pickard: We've been gratified to receive support and help from the Kingston community. We have some 100 people whom we update and sometimes ask for help. Most recently, for example, we've asked them to host 'kitchen table talks' in their homes so we can have in depth discussions of BIG with a few interested people at a time.

Most of us are long-time residents of this small city where overlapping circles ensure that word travels easily and fast. With the help of friends and acquaintances, we've reached out to and have been well received by, for example, various faith communities, organized labour organizations, continuing education groups, the francophone community, secondary school and university students and so on. In addition, here as elsewhere, coverage of basic income is increasing in all forms of media. We write and respond to letters, op-eds, interviews, etc. Interest in basic income ignites quickly as people hear of it, and small efforts on our part seem to generate unexpectedly large effects.

Benns: *In what way do you try to get this on the agenda or in the thought processes of local politicians?*

Pickard: To some extent perhaps it's simply moxie on our part. We stay in contact with the presidents of the local riding associations and meet with our elected representatives. We bring written material with us, respond to the questions and arguments put to us. We might go two by two, setting up a series of meetings. Whenever we publish op-eds and letters, we see that our local politicians get copies. We sought the support of the MPP candidates in the Provincial election last year and received it from three of the four major party candidates. Most of our local politicians have shown a real readiness to take the feasibility and potential benefits of basic income seriously.

Benns: *Do you see a basic income guarantee as replacing other social programs eventually? If so, which ones?*

Pickard: The first question is a simple one. We definitely see basic income as a replacement for provincial welfare programs. A main reason BIG is so badly needed is that our welfare programs are dysfunctional. They are humiliating, stingy, and mean spirited; they create enormous work disincentives; they trap recipients in poverty. Everyone knows this. So far, governments have tried to remedy the problems by tinkering with program details. But tinkering can't rescue fundamentally flawed programs. Basic income will not involve complex rules or the micromanagement of people's lives; access and administration will be simple; there will be total privacy and dignity for recipients who won't have to answer to any government employee for the way they use their money.

The second question is more complex. Which programs to replace depends first on having a full picture of the multiplicity of federal and provincial income support mechanisms in Canada today. We need to know the effects of closing/altering the terms of particular programs. There will surely be an ongoing need for health care, vision care, dental and drug benefits, mental health and addiction services, special assistance for people with physical or learning disabilities, etc. In addition it seems likely to be sensible to keep long established programs such as Employment Insurance and Canada Pension Plan, which have worked well in the past though recent changes may have undermined their efficacy.

Which programs to close or keep can't be discussed intelligently without access to mega data, expert analysis, and the power necessary to raise and reallocate revenues. It is government which has those resources. Once the political will to implement BIG exists, the details will have to be worked out by Government.

The immediate and downstream benefits of creating a solid income floor for everyone warrant facing this complexity and need for intra-governmental cooperation. Once in place, Basic income can have transformative power. It can restore our democracy, revitalize our economy and recreate a functioning caring Canada.

MP Scott Brison won't discount basic income guarantee; says other programs can also help with inequality

March 17, 2015

By Roderick Benns

One of the federal Liberal Party's key spokespersons on economic issues, Scott Brison, says his party won't discount the idea of implementing a basic income guarantee, but says there are other tools at a government's disposal for addressing inequality.

The Liberal Member of Parliament for Kings-Hants in Nova Scotia, Brison also serves as the Liberals' critic for finance and national revenue.

"When it all comes down to it, the issue is income inequality," says Brison, "and it's a very real problem."

"My fear is that if inequality is allowed to continue and deepen, it increasingly affects equality of opportunity, too. There will be more people who are born into economic advantage versus people who aren't," causing deepening harm to families and to society, says Brison, who also serves as vice-chair of the House of Commons standing committee on finance.

He tells *Leaders and Legacies* the social and economic consequences of inequality are catastrophic. As well, he is concerned about the trends as shown by a recent study from the Canadian Imperial Bank of Commerce. The study shows that job quality has fallen to its lowest level in more than 20 years. The data — over 25 years' — worth shows the growth of part-time work versus full-time work, self-employment versus traditional paid work, and trends in compensation packages.

While noting he is whole-heartedly committed to reducing income inequality, Brison wouldn't say whether he favours a basic income guarantee, saying the Liberals are not "espousing a specific path right now."

Instead, he points to two existing tools already at a government's disposal — the Child Tax Benefit and the Working Income Tax Benefit, for the working poor. He says these two measures alone - if properly funded — would go a long way to reducing inequality in Canada.

"So there are ways we can achieve a positive effect, even within our existing tax system."

Although Brison is not committing to a basic income guarantee, the Liberal Party itself has laid some groundwork, should they choose to go this route.

At a recent Liberal policy convention, resolution number 97 (Basic Income Supplement: Testing a Dignified Approach to Income Security for Working-age Canadians) and resolution number 100 (Creating a Basic Annual Income to be Designed and Implemented for a Fair Economy), were both adopted by federal Liberal delegates.

This has long-time Liberal heavyweights, like Senator Art Eggleton, very happy.

"I take some delight in what happened at the Liberal convention in the spring," Eggleton previously told *Leaders and Legacies*. "And when I recently saw Justin (Trudeau) I reminded him of that — and I told him he should promise" that Liberals will make this a reality.

Brison says serious consideration of a basic income guarantee in Canada can be traced as far back as the late 1960s, when Conservative leader Robert Stanfield promised to give it his attention if elected.

During this same timeframe, at a Conservative policy convention in 1969, a keen 19-year-old named Hugh Segal first learned about the idea of basic income guarantee. It is a cause the former senator has never let go of, becoming the Tories' standard bearer on this issue.

Even into the 1980s, the Macdonald commission – famous for its endorsement of free trade – also recommended a basic income guarantee. While Brian Mulroney's government took up the cause of free trade, making it their signature issue, the recommendation of a basic income guarantee was not seized upon.

Basic income and 'consensual capitalism': Tim Ellis

March 21, 2015

Roderick Benns recently interviewed Tim Ellis about a basic income guarantee. Ellis is a writer, producer, and communications consultant living in Toronto, Ontario. He serves on the executive committee of the NDP in his riding, and at this time is also the leader of the communications team for Basic Income Canada Network. Views expressed here are his own.

Benns: *How did you come to be involved with the issue of a basic income guarantee? What drives you to advocate for it?*

Ellis: I spent the first 30 years of my life in the US, and I was heavily involved in the health care debates of Obama's first term. When I moved to Canada in 2012, I knew I wanted to get involved politically on a similar level and I was looking for issues to get behind.

I'm fascinated by economics and have worked in finance, and I'm also a Millennial and living with the consequences of what we've been left from previous generations, so I'm keenly aware of how trends such as automation and outsourcing (aided by decades of neo-liberal policies) are reducing the value of labour on the market and driving a decoupling of wages from productivity.

In my quest for a way to address that issue, I stumbled across an article by former Conservative Senator Hugh Segal in which he explained a basic income. It piqued my interest, so I wrote to his office and he put me in touch with BICN, with whom I volunteer to this day.

I advocate for a basic income because I recognize that it makes both ethical and economic sense. An economy that is widely split between the haves and have-nots is bad for both classes; without sufficient demand from the consumer base, even the most successful capital-holder can't earn on his or her investments. With the declining value of labour on the market, wages are no longer sufficient to get money into the hands of consumers. A basic income addresses that issue in the simplest, most effective, and most equitable fashion. Ethically speaking, of course, it's perfectly aligned with Canadian values. We build a better society for all when we take care of each other. This is fundamental to the Canadian experience. Humans are a social species; taking care of each other has been the foundation of our success for thousands of years.

Benns: *What about a basic income guarantee makes it a social justice issue?*

Ellis: Any labour market that is predicated on the threat of suffering for failure to work is inherently coercive – and when that market then fails to deliver sufficient jobs, we all share in the blame for the suffering those results. A basic income gives people real agency in their own lives, and real leverage when negotiating with employers. On top of that, one of the great virtues of capitalism is that it drives efficiency; however, one person's efficiency is another person's layoff slip. These are very real, very human costs that we all bear. Basic income is the key to building a truly consensual capitalism that allows us to retain the virtues of the market side of our economy while still looking after the human beings that are, after all, the reason for the whole thing.

A basic income also re-prioritizes what we mean by "work." As it stands, you're only compensated for work the market values and that can deliver a profit for somebody. This means such essential and cherished human endeavours — parenting, leisure time with family and friends, engaging in art or play for the sheer joy of it, and so on — are tallied up as costs, not assets. These are the very heart of the human experience, and a basic income allows those who wish to contribute these essential assets to our society to do so without being punished for it.

Finally, I think there's a huge mental health cost that our current structure imposes on our children. We're creating a society that has adapted to constantly competing and to live in constant fear that it could, in turn, all be taken away. Kids go into deep debt to attend university for degrees that might not even get them a job, almost certainly not a job in the field they want, and all the while they know that the penalty for failure is grinding poverty and constant suffering. I don't know what percentage of my peers suffer from crippling, daily anxiety, but it's substantial. I refuse to believe that we simply need to accept constant fear and anxiety as the price of progress. I am so incredibly proud of our species. We are more than workers. We are more than consumers. And we need not live in fear.

Benns: *The most common concern is about implementing a basic income guarantee is that too many of us would choose not to work. Why do you believe this won't be the case?*

Ellis: The simple answer is the evidence. Unpaid work is fundamental to the human experience. Hobbies, volunteer hours, church and community groups, raising families – that's all work! It's just not valued by the market because there's no profit in it. But it's valued by people, and so it gets done. Financial compensation is far from the only motivation for human endeavour. We already have several examples of a basic income being secured — the most relevant and most frequently cited in Canada is the 'Mincome' pilot project in Dauphin, Manitoba — and the results routinely indicate that people either continue to work or choose to spend more time on valuable investments in the future such as education and child-rearing.

But let's dive a little further on this one for a moment. When I was a kid, we had a rotary phone at my house. Today, my smart phone has more power than the entire Apollo project — all of NASA's computational power, in my pocket! People in my generation view total automation as an inevitability. Maybe it will take a thousand years, maybe a hundred, but it's coming. And when it does, what then? Are we going to have the machines assign us busy-work so we can keep earning paycheques to scrape out a minimum-wage living? We're already seeing a huge decoupling between productivity and wages, we're already seeing ten or twenty people being able to do the work that used to take thousands. In any rational society, the premise 'less work that people need to do' would be a good thing and should free up people to pursue their own dreams. Instead, because we've tied survival to an outdated wage-based model, we get people 'freed' from their careers and immediately forced to chase after whatever work remains, no matter how bad it is, just to stay alive. Why is that a smart arrangement? How does society benefit from that?

Benns: *When you imagine Canadian life with this policy in place — say 10 years of a basic income guarantee — what does the country look like? How has it changed?*

Ellis: Existing trends towards contract labour rather than traditional employment have greatly accelerated, as the precariousness that used to be associated with these more efficient models has been drastically reduced. Small businesses have flourished — a reliable supply of capital to the consumer base has created a much more viable environment for businesses to work within at the same time that freedom from the coercive need to work in highly demanding yet extremely underpaid positions has allowed individuals to go into business for themselves as entrepreneurs. The result is a dynamic local economy.

Public health outcomes have begun to improve sharply, as people are able to access preventative care and as they live without constant anxiety imposing a draining and damaging 'fight or flight' mentality. As a result, health care costs have begun to swing downward, just as predicted by the health care organizations that led the way in recognizing a basic income as a crucial investment.

Political engagement has increased, as people feel more directly invested in the political and social system. Basic income is one of the few issues that unites the political spectrum (something that is already true). Political activism remains lively, but without the same sense of alienation and desperation that had for so long set upper and lower classes artificially against one another.

Where so many for so long had seen only a ceiling, now there is a firm floor on which to stand for themselves – and the sky is the limit.

Basic income guarantee: scrutinizing the link between work and pay

March 24 2015

Roderick Benns recently interviewed Luc Gosselin, a member of Basic Income Earth Network, and a member of France's Mouvement français pour le revenu de base, about a basic income guarantee.

Benns: *How did you come to be involved in this issue?*

Gosselin: It's the last stage in a mental voyage that started with an aphorism I coined when a teenager: Il n'y a pas de salaire pour l'ennui, which translates as: No salary is high enough to pay for boredom. A few years later, in one of Buckminster Fuller's book, I came across this:

"We should do away with the absolutely specious notion that everybody has to earn a living. It is a fact today that one in ten thousand of us can make a technological breakthrough capable of supporting all the rest. The youth of today are absolutely right in recognizing this nonsense of earning a living. We keep inventing jobs because of this false idea that everybody has to be employed at some kind of drudgery because, according to Malthusian Darwinian theory he must justify his right to exist. So we have inspectors of inspectors and people making instruments for inspectors to inspect inspectors. The true business of people should be to go back to school and think about whatever it was they were thinking about before somebody came along and told them they had to earn a living."

My little aphorism and this great quotation intermingled and I developed the fantasy that if I'd been guaranteed an income that would be enough to live on, I'd happily pay 50 percent tax on all my earnings on top of that. I seldom shared that dream of mine, but it stayed in my mind for years and years.

And then, approximately fifteen years ago, I heard an interview with Philippe Van Parijs on Radio-Canada about the concept of basic income (which he calls: allocation universelle). That was exactly my dream! I had a sort of Big Bang moment! I bought one of his books, subscribed to Basic Income Earth Network's (BIEN) newsletter and later to Basic Income Canada Network's newsletter as well, read a few other books on the subject, and talked about it on all occasions given any pretext.

The current stretch of that journey started in February 2014. I was quitting a job and getting into what I call an 'auto sabbatical leave of undefined length.' I thought it was time for me to put my time where my mouth was on that basic income business: I became a member of BIEN, attended its conference and general assembly in June, became a member of France's Mouvement français pour le revenu de base, created a Facebook Page, co-founded Revenu de base Québec, started networking with other groups in Québec and Canada.

It has become my main occupation.

Benns: *What about a basic income guarantee makes it a social justice issue?*

Gosselin: First and foremost, it would, at least, alleviate poverty and, hopefully, end it all together. It's just plain scandalous that we have not succeeded in doing that in our rich societies, that we keep treating the poor as 'pariahs.' That's why it's urgent to implement basic income, but it's not the only reason we should do it. Precariousness is spreading; it's becoming an undesirable way of life for a lot of people. Inequality polarizes our societies and causes a deep feeling of intolerable injustice. Both precariousness and inequality will become very important problems, and dangerous ones to the point of fomenting rebellion, if we don't take care. There are numerous and complicated causes for that situation; political and economic solutions come from right and left in a cacophony of dogmas that leaves one deaf. Basic income is a solution worth careful attention in order to solve, or at least reduce, those social injustices. I've come to think that discussing it is the most important thing that we need to do in our society, nowadays. And it's a focus that would unite us.

Many social justice issues would have to be taken into account in our discussion of basic income: first, as mentioned, we would have to question seriously the way we treat the poor, and anybody who goes through hard times in life for that matter; the link between work and pay would have to be scrutinized; the value of a great lot of unpaid work would be recognized and enhanced; solidarity and community, equality and liberty would get new and deeper meanings; just to mention a few things that come to my mind.

I'm not a specialist of social issues, but I can't help seeing basic income as the main social issue of the 21st century, because it encompasses many of the most important ones.

Benns: *The most common concern is about implementing a basic income guarantee is that too many of us would choose not to work. Why do you believe this won't be the case?*

Gosselin: It has not been the case in any of the projects that I know of where basic income has been implemented for a limited time: India, Namibia, Dauphin (Manitoba), London (UK), South-Carolina, Alaska.

The people I know who work with recipients of social assistance tell me that a majority of them want to work. We all know what happens when they do: not only do they pay the highest income tax possible, 100 percent, when they reach a ridiculously small amount of supplementary income on top of their allowances, but they have to go through a maze of paperwork to report on it and they are treated as suspects of fraud anyway. It's no way to encourage work. Unconditional basic income would solve that.

And then, there is that well known experiment: when asked how many of their fellow citizens would stop working if they had basic income, people say that around 80 percent would do so; and if asked what they would do themselves, most of them say they would keep on working. It's a matter of false perception.

Benns: *When you imagine Canadian life with this policy in place — say 10 or 20 years of the basic income guarantee — what does the country look like? How has it changed?*

Gosselin: I imagine it will look more like a democracy. We would have gone through such a turmoil of conversations, discussions and debates on the way to its implementation that we would keep them going, hopefully.

Back to liberté, égalité, fraternité, at long last!

Canadians would be healthier, more socially engaged with a basic income: Julia Endicott

April 3, 2015

Roderick Benns recently interviewed Julia Endicott about her advocacy for a basic income guarantee. Endicott is a first year Bachelor of Education student at Queen's University. She also holds a Bachelor of Science from the University of Waterloo and a Masters of Chemistry from the University of Toronto.

Benns: *From what perspective do you approach this issue? And, how did you come to be involved?*

Endicott: I have always been interested in social justice and I believe wealth inequality and poverty are issues that can be addressed if people can be inspired act. I learned about the Kingston Action Group for a Basic Income Guarantee when Toni Pickard did a guest lecture in a class I am taking as part of my Bachelor of Education at Queen's University. I had heard of the idea before but Toni's description of the group and the type of activism they were doing made me excited to get involved with them.

Benns: *What about a basic income guarantee makes it a social justice issue?*

Endicott: The United Nations declaration of human rights says that everyone has the right to an adequate standard of living. In our current system this right is not possible for many people. A basic income would recognize this right and change the way we look at food and shelter, they aren't privileges that you have to work for but rights that everyone should have. One goal of many social justice movements is the eradication of poverty. One of the things that drew me to the idea of a basic income is is the fact that it has a real chance of eliminating poverty. Poverty intersects with so many other forms of oppression that by addressing poverty we would also be making our society more equitable in terms of race, gender, and many other areas of injustice.

Benns: *In what way would this policy show there is real value in raising a family?*

Endicott: A basic income guarantee would partially be a recognition of the value of all the unpaid work that is done. The most obvious example of this is valuing the work of parents (often women) who stay home with their children. One of the things that I find so ridiculous about our economic system is that over the last 30 years as efficiency and productivity have steadily increased it has become impossible for most families to survive off of the full-time employment income of one adult.

By providing an income while parents are not working, the basic income guarantee shows that this type of work is valued. It should be noted however that a basic income would be an income floor and that things like parental leaves and employment insurance would still be needed to allow people to maintain their standard of living. Since a basic income is unconditional it would also benefit people other than parents such as artists, students, volunteers, and people caring for their elders who do valuable though unpaid work in our communities.

Benns: *When you imagine Canadian life with this policy in place — say 10 or 20 years of a basic income guarantee — what does the country look like? How has it changed?*

Endicott: I see a place where the people are happier, healthier, and more engaged. Government spending required for health care and the criminal justice system has been significantly reduced and the savings are being used to continue funding a basic income guarantee. I think there will be more small businesses and more entrepreneurs because people will have a solid safety net to fall back on.

As jobs have started to disappear in manufacturing and other industries due to automation people have used their basic income to allow them to transition to other forms of employment. One way to see what a strong effect a basic income can have on poverty levels in our future is to look at the case of seniors and the huge effect of OAS/GIS on reducing poverty amongst seniors. More people will be able to study subjects that interest them rather than what they think they need to be the most employable.

There is still a divide between rich and poor and most people are employed full time to pay for their desires but everyone has enough to cover their needs. This to me is the most important thing about this policy — everyone has the ability to live with dignity making our society as a whole stronger.

Everyone should benefit from the prosperity of a society: Jonathan Brun

April 8, 2015

Roderick Benns recently interviewed Jonathan Brun about basic income. Brun is a metallurgical engineer by training, and has actively built various Internet companies. He has worked with the Basic Income Canada Network to advocate for the policy in Quebec.

Benns: *How did you come to be involved in this issue? What makes you advocate for it?*

Brun: Basic Income came to my attention through the recent Swiss referendum, to be held in 2016. As well, a number of technologists and entrepreneurs have begun to speak about basic income as a way to support entrepreneurship. This led me to meet with experts on the subject, such as Jurgen De Wispelare of McGill University.

Since my introduction, I have worked with the Basic Income Canada Network and we also started a citizen initiative for Québec, titled Revenu de base Québec. We hope to put the issue on the map as a solution to social justice, entrepreneurship and government simplification.

Benns: *What about a basic income guarantee makes it a social justice issue?*

Brun: Justice is a complex subject, but the main path towards a just society is one in which individuals are empowered and free. Basic Income can help provide independence to people, allowing them to pursue their dreams, reduce their financial constraints and fight for justice. Without freedom, there cannot be justice and without a floor under each person's feet, there cannot be freedom.

Benns: *The most common concern is that by implementing a basic income guarantee that too many of us would choose not to work. Why do you believe this won't be the case?*

Brun: Certain jobs will disappear or the salaries will be forced to increase to compensate for poor working conditions. Low wage jobs such as the service industry will likely suffer, but this will force companies to innovate and increase the value of the service they offer. With increased labour costs due to their bargaining power, automation will be accelerated, further freeing us to pursue economic activity that reflects the full potential of the human mind.

Ultimately, we all want fulfilling work with reasonable working hours. A basic income will free people to pursue work and start companies that will in turn push innovation and society forward. A basic income should be based on the prosperity of a society, much like a dividend. As we increase the economic prosperity and efficiency of our society, the returns on that success should be distributed to the people who form the society – creating a feedback loop that will propel us forward and align our interests.

The revolutions of the 18th and 19th centuries in Europe and the Americas freed millions of people from tyranny and bondage, this led to the longest period of growth and improvement in human history. To reboot the economy and continue to grow, we must engage in an emancipation of the same magnitude.

Renowned economist says the 'Precariat' is an entirely new class of people that wants to eliminate itself

April 13, 2015

By Roderick Benns

The combination of people in short-term and contract jobs and those in other precarious work and living situations, has grown into a massive new class of people. Named the 'Precariat' by renowned economist Guy Standing, he says it is the only class of people in the history of the world that wants to eliminate itself.

Speaking in Toronto recently to support his latest book, *Precariat Charter: From Denizens to Citizens*, Standing told an energized crowd that he estimates the Precariat class is approaching 40 percent in Canada.

Standing observes that precariousness is becoming the new normal after years of neo-liberal policies that have broken down the old order. (Neo-liberalism emphasizes privatization, deregulation, and globalization — the so-called right wing policies that promote a laissez-faire atmosphere for economic development.)

"The Precariat is becoming stronger every day. It is a radical class," he tells those assembled, "because it is the only one that wants to abolish itself. That makes it very dangerous."

Standing believes the Precariat could create new volatility within the social fabric because these people have no real voice. This could lead to the kind of zealotry that can see the quick rise of extremist political parties.

The Precariat is desired by global capitalism, says Standing, because the "systematic dismantling of social solidarity" benefits capitalists immensely.

The economist says the Precariat itself is characterized by three dimensions:

1. The Precariat has to rely only on money wages instead of non-wage benefits, rights-based benefits, or community benefits.
2. The Precariat is losing civil, political, and economic rights. Citizens are becoming denizens – nothing more than inhabitants of space.
3. People within the Precariat have no sense of occupational identity or narrative. They are the first, mass class in history whose level of education is above the level of labour they are expected to perform.

To get the Precariat reengaged in society, he proposes a new framework – a charter of 29 actions that should be taken in order to give the Precariat and frailer members of society better access to basic rights.

One of the foremost among these 29 points is that people should receive a basic income, which could be topped up through earned incomes. Seen as an ethical justification, Standing also sees it as a "social dividend derived from our forebears' investments and hard work."

A basic income guarantee and other 'charter' rights can only be manifested through the "struggle for representation," he says.

"It's needed more across nations – the voices (of the Precariat) are needed within government. And that's only beginning here," he says, referring to both Western Europe, Canada and the U.S.

Standing says a basic income guarantee is an "ethical demand for justice, even ahead of poverty."

"We must set up capital funds for the redistribution of basic income. It's so important that youth – which has such great energy – mobilize and fight" for this.

Standing says the 18-month pilot that he was involved with in India, in which thousands of men, women and children were provided with unconditional monthly cash payments, saw improvement in their lives across the board. He says people wanted to work more, not less, once poverty was taken off the table.

While acknowledging there will always be a small percentage who won't work, Standing says that overall it's "an insult to the human condition" to believe that most people won't stay active once they realize a scarcity mentality is no longer necessary.

During his talk in Toronto, the economist was asked by an audience member how to get more involved in advocating for the rights-based issues he spells out in his latest book, including a basic income. Standing pointed out that the Basic Income Canada Network is very active and would welcome more Canadians' engagement.

"I have spoken in many parts of Canada and I can feel the energy around this issue here," he says.

Whether you're left or right, Hugh Segal believes a basic income guarantee just makes good sense

April 23, 2015

By Roderick Benns

Hugh Segal is the Master of Massey College. He is also a Canadian political strategist, author, commentator, academic, and former Conservative senator. He served as chief of staff to Ontario Premier Bill Davis and Canadian Prime Minister Brian Mulroney. Segal is a former Vice-Chair of the Senate Subcommittee on Urban Poverty and has promoted a basic income guarantee since 1969.

There's a reason the issue of a basic income guarantee never seems to go away, says retired Conservative Senator Hugh Segal — the idea simply makes too much sense.

Basic income (also called a guaranteed annual income) would see any Canadian who falls below the poverty line topped up with enough money to cover a basic living standard. Almost all models for basic income implementation would see it replace provincial welfare systems.

Segal says there are three things driving the support for this policy change.

"The first one is that we have a core understanding now that the gap between the rich and those living in poverty is not getting smaller. In fact, it's getting substantially larger. And that is destabilizing for everyone, including for the economic forces that require our economy to work," he says.

Using the language of economist Guy Standing, Segal says those in precarious work situations – dubbed the 'Precariat' – coupled with people in low paying jobs, usually without benefits, creates the need for such a basic income policy.

"The second reason" that a basic income guarantee remains a viable idea, "is despite the billions we spend on social transfers to the provinces, the core issue is that the three million Canadians living in poverty is not changing. There is simply not enough meaningful change," on this issue, says Segal.

Segal points to the experience of the Guaranteed Annual Supplement for seniors that was passed in 1975 by Ontario Premier Bill Davis. At the time, Segal was a 25-year-old legislative assistant who remembers a transformative decision that was made for Ontario's seniors.

"Seniors were in deep difficulty – they were buying cat and dog food to augment their diets. The Toronto Star documented this," he recalls. The Davis government decided to ensure cash transfers for seniors would happen each month, and the tax system was the chosen delivery instrument.

"Their incomes were automatically topped up. For seniors, it worked wonderfully. Poverty went from 35 percent in this population to three percent. The policy spread across the country and became federalized."

Segal points out that this simple system is all that basic income policy is – topping up those who need it so they don't fall below the poverty line. If they do fall below, this can lead to all kinds of expensive health issues, he notes.

The third reason the basic income idea continues to gain traction, says Segal, is that "we know that if we put our heads together, we don't have to accept a hodgepodge of programs. Welfare doesn't support anyone — it ensnares and entangles. It creates judgment. It is deeply problematic, wasteful, and expensive."

Segal says a basic income guarantee should not be about left wing-right wing politics.

"Whether left or right, this idea is attractive for all. Just give the money to the people living in poverty who will know what to do with it."

Most people in poverty are already working — they just don't earn enough: Segal

May 1, 2015

By Roderick Benns

Most Canadians living in poverty are not sitting around, says a retired Conservative senator — they are actually working. They're just not earning enough to adequately get by.

That's a problem for Hugh Segal, who has spent over 40 years in pursuit of a basic income guarantee policy for Canadians.

"There is no evidence that people living beneath the poverty line in Canada won't choose to work" with a basic income guarantee. "In fact we know that about 70 percent of people who happen to live beneath poverty line are working — they just don't earn enough."

Segal says some people have two jobs, given the precarious nature of work, as they try to balance various commitments of part-time hours. With a basic income guarantee, a simple assessment at tax time would ensure they would be brought up to the poverty line, complete with tax incentives to keep people working.

"It has to be structured as a top up — that's the way to make it work well."

When he considers provincial welfare systems, Segal is adamant they need to go.

"Most welfare programs make it impossible to work. If you earn more than $200 a month and receive welfare in Ontario, for instance, they start clawing money back. There are so many disincentives to work," he says. "With basic income, it's an automatic top-up of a basic amount to live."

While the federal Conservative government created the work Working Income Tax Benefit, which pays benefits to single persons and families, including an additional amount to working people with disabilities, Segal points out it's poorly funded. In 2012 the benefit sat at a maximum of $970 for a single worker per year ($1,762 for a family) and gets cut off at the net income of $17,478 (or $26,952 for a family).

According to Statistics Canada, Canada has one of the highest proportions of low-paid workers among similarly industrialized countries (25 percent). This is higher than in European countries and similar to the American rate.

Goodbye welfare, hello basic income

May 1, 2015

By Roderick Benns

Inequality is having a catastrophic effect on the U.S. economy, on the American social fabric, and in the health of its people. We are not immune, here in Canada. We are merely in a slower free fall. Inequality is not an issue for poor people – it is an issue for all of us.

The Basic Income solution

There is a movement that has been gaining steam in Canada to help halt this slide toward a more unequal and less healthy society. What Canada needs is a basic income guarantee as its next great social program. In some ways, it's incredibly simple. No person in Canada would ever fall below a set, annual income threshold.

For our purposes here, let's say that cut-off is $20,000 a year. In one example, a man may be employed part time while also attending college for some re-training and he earns $12,000 a year. The basic income guarantee would kick in with $8,000 at tax time, spread out monthly using our existing and effective tax delivery system.

In another example, a single mom stays home to care for her children and volunteers part-time in her community. She would be entitled to $20,000 so she doesn't slip below the poverty line.

This is not living the good life. This is a 'basic income' to meet her needs. This is far better than punitive welfare, where she must purge herself of every asset that she has. In the welfare model, she must also never earn more at a job than $200 a month (in Ontario) or she will see money clawed back.

In other words, she must be completely impoverished, and then be expected to somehow start again. This is not a social program; it is a neo-liberal monstrosity. And it is ineffective in the extreme.

PEI to lead the way?

After all party leaders in Prince Edward Island endorsed a Basic Income Guarantee (BIG) program recently as a poverty reduction strategy, there is optimism that the long-sought-after program might just become a reality in Canada's smallest province. That's a great start.

The biggest elephant in the room is a fear that a large cross-section of people will simply stop being productive if they have a basic income guarantee. But there is ample evidence to suggest this simply won't happen, from experiments done in Dauphin, Manitoba in the 1970s, Brazil in 2004 (and ongoing), a two-year pilot in Namibia from 2008-2010, and India in 2011, among other examples. Speaking about the most recent India experiment, renowned economist Guy Standing said that people worked more, not less.

A better life

When one is overly preoccupied with paying the rent on time, it leaves little room for daring to dream about other opportunities, to innovate and better oneself, or to even simply do an attentive job of raising a family. If we take the worry of poverty off people's shoulders, there's a much better chance to create a richer, more meaningful society for everyone.

When a Senate committee made rough calculations six years ago, they found it would cost about $20 billion to implement such a program. A 2008 study, estimated that $72 billion to $86 billion was the cost of health care, criminal justice and lost productivity, all associated with the crippling effects of inequality. In other words, we would actually be saving money to implement a basic income guarantee.

As for paying for such a program, it's obvious that the entire welfare system could eventually be scrapped to save money. Other big-ticket and costly programs could be analyzed for their effectiveness or need once a basic income was part of Canadian life.

Those who lean left on the political spectrum can appreciate the obvious goal of ending poverty for all. Even those on the far right hand side of political opinion, who may only wish to talk about economic models, should appreciate a more simplified tax code, far less bureaucracy, and a chance for all Canadians to have more money to spend toward our economy.

Unlike our southern neighbour, Canada began as an egalitarian nation of modest means. We didn't have a dominant upper class — we just had people working together in common cause.

Let's choose a common cause again.

The toleration of inequality is a continuing blight on our national legacy, in a country where we should have a democratic right to equity. Canada has been blessed with a legacy of great leaders. It will be great leadership again — at national, provincial, and community levels — that creates an equitable society of opportunity for all.

Calgary Mayor Naheed Nenshi vows to take 'leadership' on basic income guarantee

May 9, 2015

By Roderick Benns

Calgary Mayor Naheed Nenshi called for "brave steps" in the fight against inequality and vowed to take leadership on pushing for a basic income guarantee.

Speaking to a National Poverty Reduction Summit in Ottawa on May 7, Nenshi told a capacity crowd that it's up to Canada's mayors to take leadership on important issues, like reducing poverty.

"The frustrating thing is that we know what the answers are."

Bringing up the idea of a guaranteed annual income (or basic income guarantee) – and noting that this is just an extension of the Child Tax Credit, except that it would be for all Canadians who might drop below the poverty line – Nenshi called for courage from politicians to take steps to deal with poverty.

Pointing to his own immigrant family's roots, he says he has lived experience of poverty. "Like many immigrant families, we worked hard and had times of struggle. The core of our success as a nation is that we are all in this together. We need to look after one another."

The first Muslim mayor of a major North American city, Nenshi's parents came from Tanzania. Nenshi was awarded the 'World Mayor' prize in 2014 by the City Mayors Foundation and was the first Canadian mayor to win this award.

The mayor's comments come on the heels of a provincial election in Prince Edward Island in which all parties supported the advancement of a basic income guarantee. The Liberal government under Wade MacLauchlan (who won the election) went so far as to call for a model program, not just a pilot, with potential for long-term established benefits:

"We'd be actively interested in pursuing that (Basic Income Guarantee)...I'd call it a model program and build in a commitment to evidence-based research and action-based research," he said at an all-candidate's debate.

Sheila Regehr, chair of the Basic Income Canada Network, says it is "very exciting" to hear about Nenshi taking leadership on the issue of a basic income guarantee.

"I hope his colleagues in municipalities across Canada will engage with him. Certainly they are the order of government closest to people and face, first-hand, the problems that gaps in income security create for their communities, she says."

Regehr points out there is solid evidence of the individual and community-level benefits of a basic income, from Dauphin, Manitoba in the 1970s, through international programs, to current Canadian research on the wellbeing of seniors and families with children who receive guaranteed incomes.

"The Basic Income Canada Network hopes more Canadians, like Mayor Nenshi, will realize that the foundation is already built. He described this as a brave step — and it is also a smart one," says Regehr.

Canada ready for a basic income revolution

May 22, 2015

By Roderick Benns

A CBC story this week highlighted that more than three-quarters of the world's workforce have insecure, part-time, or temporary jobs, according to the International Labour Organization. That means that only 25 percent of the world's population is doing stable, full-time work.

For a made-in-Canada example, the Toronto Star reports on research findings this week that in the Greater Toronto Area, about 52 percent of workers are in temporary, contract, or part-time positions.

There are all kinds of reasons for precarious employment, from automation, to a surplus of labour in developing countries, to new information technologies. This is a clock that cannot be turned back. Labour unions can fight all they want but there is simply not enough 'work' as it is now defined to go around.

Given the rapidly changing structures in employment around the world, it is not exaggeration to say this is a revolutionary time. Why, then, are we not calling for a revolutionary response?

It's time for politicians to lead. It's time to stop consulting opinion polls and start consulting top civil servants to direct them to look at the merits of a basic income guarantee policy. The best way to counter chronic, precarious employment is to ensure no one slips below the poverty line during this worldwide transition.

Canada, like most of the world, can no longer count on traditional job growth to lift people out of poverty and into the middle class. Increasingly, the middle class itself is becoming more insecure. That's why Canada needs a basic income guarantee as its next great social program. By ensuring the state keeps people out of poverty by providing a basic income with minimal conditions (instead of welfare), we can ensure that everyone has an income sufficient to meet their basic needs and live with dignity, regardless of their work status. (Basic income is known by many names, whether basic income, guaranteed income, livable income, or minimum income. What's important is the concept, not the name.)

Fortunately, there are numerous examples from around the world, including Canada, where some form of basic income has been tried.

- In part of Namibia where an unconditional basic income grant was tried, child malnutrition dropped from 42 percent to 10 per cent, and during this time there was close to zero dropouts from school.
- In a World Bank study, researchers gave cash transfers to families in Malawi and ended up increasing school attendance of females with the program because they could afford to go to school to better themselves and their families.
- In eight villages in India, every man, woman, and child was given a modest amount of cash money with no strings attached. Economist Guy Standing, who was involved with the project, reports there were many benefits, including – but not limited to – improved housing, latrines, walls and roofs, better nutrition, better health outcomes, improved school attendance, and more empowerment for those with disabilities.

Some small-scale investments also happened, such as more and better seeds for farmers, sewing machines, the establishment of small shops, repairs to equipment, and more.

"Contrary to the skeptics," writes Standing, "the grants led to more labour and work...There was a shift from casual wage labour to more...self-employed farming and business activity, with less distress...Women gained more than men."

The important thing, Standing argues, is that families took action themselves and didn't need to be told by the State how to spend their money to take care of themselves.

As study after study in Canada and around the world shows that labour markets are shrinking and inequality is rising, it is paramount that we act to safeguard our people from precarious work environments that are now the norm.

Prince Edward Island Premier Wade MacLauchlan agreed to begin a basic income guarantee program for residents during the recent election campaign. His recent win puts PEI in a leadership position on this issue in Canada.

Calgary Mayor Naheed Nenshi says it's time for a guaranteed annual income, which makes him Canada's key municipal leader on this issue. Federally, only the Green Party has taken a clear, supportive stand on this issue.

A new social order has been thrust upon us. Let's take some initiative, seize the moment, and show the world how progressive social policy can be done.

Calgary's Mayor Nenshi to try to partner with other mayors to push for basic income

May 25, 2015

By Roderick Benns

Calgary Mayor Naheed Nenshi will focus on building support for a basic income guarantee with other mayors across Canada.

Nenshi made headlines earlier this month at the National Poverty Reduction Summit in Ottawa when he called for "brave steps" in the fight against inequality. He vowed to take leadership on pushing for a basic income guarantee.

Now, *Leaders and Legacies* has learned through Nenshi's communications adviser, Daorcey Le Bray, that the mayor seems intent on building support for a basic income guarantee through his fellow mayors from across Canada.

"Although he spoke about it (basic income) during the speech, we're going to wait for another time to start really banging the drum on this, likely in partnership with other mayors," says Le Bray in an email exchange with *Leaders and Legacies*.

Le Bray says while there is no formal campaign at this time, "the mayor will continue to raise this issue with colleagues from across the country."

Speaking to a capacity crowd at the poverty reduction summit earlier this month, Nenshi said that it's up to Canada's mayors to take leadership on important issues, like reducing poverty.

Time to start treating our own citizens as well as we do corporations: Hugh Segal

May 26, 2015

By Roderick Benns

A former Canadian Conservative senator, Hugh Segal, says it's time to start treating Canadian citizens as well as corporations.

Segal, who has spent over 40 years in pursuit of a basic income guarantee policy for Canadians, says the nature of work is shifting and governments need to respond. A basic income would see any Canadian who falls below the poverty line topped up with enough money to cover a basic living standard. Almost all models for basic income implementation would see it replace provincial welfare systems.

"The nature of work guarantees is changing. At one time, a Grade 12 education in Canada meant solid work in the mines, the forestry industry, tourism, and so on — but those days are gone. They are gone in other countries too," he tells *Leaders and Legacies.*

What they are being replaced with, says Segal, is "something more precarious," citing the work of economist Guy Standing. People are doing more work for themselves, says Segal, and they're trying to balance more projects. He sees a basic income guarantee as a plug for people, "to stop all the water from leaving the drain."

Segal points to the events leading up to the 2008 financial crisis, led by the U.S., which had worldwide implications.

"There was a lot of gaming of the system in Wall Street in the US. Then what we (wealthy countries) did is we raised hundreds of billions of dollars from taxpayers to provide liquidity" to bail everyone out.

Segal says he believes that money was needed in the system to help prevent a deepening economic crisis, so he wasn't opposed to the steps needed to fix it — even with the evidence of unfair game playing that caused the situation in the first place.

"What I wonder, though, is why we're not prepared to find liquidity and support for individuals? If we can find the money to do it for the big guys, then we can for other folks, too," says Segal, in reference to providing basic income support.

In a previous interview with *Leaders and Legacies*, Segal noted that "if we put our heads together, we don't have to accept a hodgepodge of programs. Welfare doesn't support anyone — it ensnares and entangles. It creates judgment. It is deeply problematic, wasteful, and expensive."

He says a basic income guarantee should not be about left wing or right wing politics. "Whether left or right, this idea is attractive for all. Just give the money to the people living in poverty who will know what to do with it."

Edmonton Mayor Don Iveson speaks out in favour of a basic income guarantee

June 1, 2015

By Roderick Benns

Edmonton Mayor Don Iveson says the "evidence is overwhelming" for providing a basic income guarantee for Canadians — and he thinks his city and Calgary are great places to try out pilot projects.

On the heels of a national poverty conference in Ottawa, in which Calgary Mayor Naheed Nenshi voiced his support for a basic income guarantee, Edmonton's Iveson says not only is he in favour of the policy, he thinks Alberta's two largest cities should work with the Province to figure out how to make it happen.

"We (Edmonton and Calgary) may be in a position to pilot some different solutions. As partners, we may be able to help the Province implement" a basic income guarantee pilot.

The policy is also sometimes known as a guaranteed annual income or negative income tax. Last week, *Leaders and Legacies* learned through Nenshi's communications adviser, Daorcey Le Bray, that Calgary's mayor was intent on building support for a basic income guarantee through fellow mayors across Canada. Iveson's support — and his suggestion of pilot projects with the Province — may gel nicely with Nenshi's vision.

"This is the advantage of him (Nenshi) and me working together in Alberta. We already have ongoing discussions with the Province," says Iveson.

The task force on poverty that Iveson initiated is still considering the policies of basic income and a living wage, which are not incompatible concepts, the mayor notes. The task force will report back with their recommendations on a number of policy fronts this fall.

"It's definitely a measure we're evaluating. There is a lot of phenomenal evidence from Dauphin, Manitoba to support this. There is no doubt to me that income security is a pillar...and will be a part of our plan," he tells *Leaders and Legacies*.

A Conversation with Hugh Segal

Two days after Rachel Notley's NDP swept to power in Alberta, Iveson found himself having a conversation with former Conservative Senator, Hugh Segal, and now Master of Massey College. Segal has long been the conservative standard-bearer on basic income guarantee policy.

"I had an extraordinary conversation with him about a guaranteed annual income," recalls Iveson. Segal was proof, he says, there is a "broad coalition of people who think this is the right things to do."

The mayor says a basic income guarantee "would cut to the chase on a lot of this work" on poverty reduction. He believes it would also help the housing situation for people living in poverty, since they could then afford to have the foundational base they need for success. Iveson says he is aware the federal Liberal Party has talked about trying out pilots. As well, the Green Party also supports a form of basic income guarantee.

He notes that city leaders like him "can help move the needle on public acceptance" for such policy, given the absence of party affiliations.

Simcoe Muskoka District Health Unit becomes first in Ontario to endorse basic income

June 2, 2015

By Roderick Benns

The Simcoe Muskoka District Health Unit has become the first health unit in Ontario to officially endorse a basic income guarantee – and they're hoping they can convince their provincial counterparts to follow suit.

Associate Medical Officer of Health, Lisa Simon, says their unit committed in 2012 to focusing on the social determinants of health as the best strategy for public health advocacy. Within the social determinants list, 'income and income distribution' is the first determinant considered.

"That's why we decided we would focus on people living in low income, given the health inequities they face," said Simon.

Simon stresses that she and her board see a basic income guarantee as a "very important policy measure" to bring people out of poverty and to improve their health outcomes. She is involved with a health equity working group, where there are joint members between the Association of Local Public Health Agencies (alPHa) and the Ontario Public Health Association. After this group facilitated a panel discussion on basic income at an Ontario-wide public health conference, she then brought it to her board of health. They endorsed the concept and supported her submission of an alPHa resolution and backgrounder on this issue.

"In Ontario, at least, we're first. Certainly no one has taken it to alPHa," Simon tells *Leaders and Legacies*. The annual general meeting for alPHa is June 8, when a vote will be taken on the proposed resolution.

Within her proposal that she is hoping alPHa will adopt next week, Simon writes that alPHa officially requests "that the federal Ministers of Employment and Social Development, Labour, and Health, as well as the Ontario Ministers Responsible for the Poverty Reduction Strategy, Labour, Children and Youth Services, and Health and Long-Term Care, prioritize joint federal-provincial consideration and investigation into a basic income guarantee, as a policy option for reducing poverty and income insecurity and for providing opportunities for those in low income."

She further writes that the "Prime Minister, the Premier of Ontario, the Chief Public Health Officer, the Chief Medical Officer of Health for Ontario, the Canadian Public Health Association, the Ontario Public Health Association, the Federation of Canadian Municipalities, and the Association of Municipalities of Ontario" should also be advised of this stance.

When asked if she sees the potential adoption of the alPHa resolution as something that will get noticed and possibly help to spur policy changes, Simon struck a positive note.

"I would hope that when an organization like alPHa, representing 36 health units across Ontario...takes a position on an issue...then this should be seen" as significant.

"We provide expertise in the area of prevention and in the health of the population so when we make a policy recommendation that we feel is aligned" with these goals, "we hope it will be considered strongly," says Simon.

She adds that "as public health professionals, if it is passed by alPHa, it would show basic income is an effective way" to address poverty and respond to the social determinants of health.

Second prominent Conservative speaks out in favour of basic income pilot projects

June 9, 2015

By Roderick Benns

Retired Conservative Senator Michael Meighen says it's time for governments to set up pilot projects across Canada to give a basic income guarantee a chance as future policy.

In an interview with *Leaders and Legacies* in Toronto, Meighen says the idea is "very attractive on paper" so it will be important to follow this through with real-world testing.

"That's where pilot projects come in – we have to test it," says Meighen, who notes that if the pilots are successful, then the policy becomes easier to sell, politically.

Meighen, who is also a well-known lawyer and philanthropist, is the second prominent Tory to speak out recently about a basic income guarantee. Retired Conservative Senator Hugh Segal spoke to *Leaders and Legacies* recently about this issue, and Segal has been a long-time proponent of the policy.

Meighen points out that when he was a Conservative candidate in Montreal, running to be an MP in the elections of 1972 and 1974, he advocated for a basic income guarantee under the banner of Conservative Party leader, Robert Stanfield.

While Meighen wasn't successful in attaining a seat during those elections (and Stanfield himself never led his party to victory), the policy always struck him as something that deserved a second look.

Ontario's association of health units green lights basic income as policy

June 10, 2015

By Roderick Benns

Medical officers of health and boards of health members from across Ontario are now officially calling for provincial and federal governments to bring in a basic income guarantee – more momentum on an issue that is attracting national attention.

The Association of Local Public Health Agencies (alPHa) is a not-for-profit organization that provides leadership to the boards of health and public health units in Ontario. They voted on Monday to endorse a proposal that stemmed from the Simcoe Muskoka District Health Unit's support of basic income.

In their resolution, alPHa points out that "1,745,900 Ontarians, or 13.9 percent of the population, live in low income according to the 2011 National Household Survey after-tax low-income measure."

They define a basic income guarantee as a "cash transfer from government to citizens not tied to labour market participation," enough to ensure "everyone an income sufficient to meet basic needs and live with dignity, regardless of work status..."

The resolution also points out that basic income "resembles income guarantees currently provided in Canada for seniors and children, which have contributed to health improvements in those age groups."

Simcoe Muskoka District Health Unit's Associate Medical Officer of Health, Dr. Lisa Simon, is involved with a health equity working group, where there are joint members between alPHa and the

Ontario Public Health Association. After this group facilitated a panel discussion recently on basic income at an Ontario-wide public health conference, she then brought it to her own board of health. They endorsed the concept in Simcoe Muskoka and supported her submission of the Ontario-wide resolution and backgrounder.

Simon says her health unit committed in 2012 to focusing on the social determinants of health as the best strategy for public health advocacy. Within the social determinants list, 'income and income distribution' is the first determinant considered to ensure good health.

In an earlier interview with *Leaders and Legacies*, Simon says she is hopeful for more movement from the adoption of this proposal by alPHa.

"We provide expertise in the area of prevention and in the health of the population so when we make a policy recommendation that we feel is aligned" with these goals, "we hope it will be considered strongly," says Simon.

Segal says if Liberals put basic income in platform, it will force rivals to respond

June 11, 2015

By Roderick Benns

If there's one thing retired Conservative Senator Hugh Segal knows a thing or two about, it's political strategy. Segal was chief of staff to former Prime Minister Brian Mulroney in the 1990s and associate secretary of cabinet in Ontario in the 1980s.

So when he thinks about the Liberal Party of Canada's policy resolutions last year, about supporting a basic income guarantee, he knows how much they have potentially differentiated themselves from their main rivals.

"I think for the Liberal Party to say 'we're going to do pilot projects' is a very prudent and constructive thing to say. They're on the side of trying something new, with all the appropriate calibration and assessment," Segal tells *Leaders and Legacies*. The retired senator – and now master of Massey College – has been a long-time proponent of basic income policy.

"If it (a basic income policy) ends up in their actual platform, then that will mean the NDP and the Conservatives will have to respond."

Segal refers to the 2014 federal Liberal policy convention, where two resolutions were made and accepted by delegates that steer the party toward a basic income guarantee for working-age Canadians. However, this does not mean it will necessarily find its way into the party's platform for this fall's federal election.

Segal says that if the Liberals did put some kind of basic income guarantee in their platform, it would at least ensure the issue of poverty "will actually be discussed."

"In the 2011 election the word 'poverty' never once came up. So who has the best approach would be a great debate," he says.

When asked if he every broached the topic of basic income to Brian Mulroney's government in the early 1990s, when he was serving as Mulroney's chief of staff, Segal said indeed he had.

"Not only did I broach it, I chaired an interdepartmental committee on income security...and we looked at the means for moving in this direction."

What the government eventually decided to focus on, though, says Segal, was to "radically change the structure of family allowance, tilted toward those with greater need, and to end universality."

He points out the government was faced with an austerity mindset near the end of their reign in 1992-93. While Segal has been the most vocal Conservative proponent for basic income policy for many years, he is now being joined by another prominent retired Conservative. Distinguished philanthropist and former Senator Michael Meighen, has now also spoken out in favour of pilot projects, declaring the policy to be "very attractive on paper," and that it deserves to be tested.

Meighen advocated for a basic income guarantee under the banner of Conservative Party leader, Robert Stanfield, when he ran for office in the early 1970s.

A basic income guarantee is 'the smart thing and the right thing' to do says physician, advocate

June 19, 2015

By Roderick Benns

A Saskatoon-based physician, author, and advocate says a basic income guarantee is both "the smart thing and the right thing" to do for society.

Dr. Ryan Meili was in Kingston, Ontario, recently to talk to more than 100 people about the importance of the social determinants of health at an event that was hosted by Basic Income Kingston. The social determinants of health influence health outcomes for people and include many components that work together, including income and income distribution, education, unemployment and job security, among others.

Meili described a basic income guarantee as "an exciting opportunity" and a kind of "social investment to counter inequality," pointing out that getting people out of poverty is the first social determinant of health on the list for good reason. While there are many models for implementing a basic income guarantee, he says the most important thing is to begin the process and invest in society.

"The evidence is on the side of making social investments," he says, pointing out that Canada is in dire need of a national housing strategy as one example.

Meili is the founder of Upstream, a national, non-partisan group billed as a "movement to create a healthy society through evidence-based, people-centred ideas." Upstream is attempting to reframe public discourse around tackling the social determinants of health to improve society.

Meili is the author of *A Healthy Society: How a Focus on Health can Revive Canadian Democracy* and one of the leading Canadian advocates for more attention to be paid to the social determinants of health.

Tackling the common question of whether or not a basic income would create a work disincentive, Meili says most people want to be productive members of society.

"But when we give people just barely enough to get by," he says, citing social assistance models, it doesn't have the same kind of positive impact, either for that person or for society. He points out that in a bare bones welfare model, someone might not have enough money left over each month to be able to take a train ride to explore new employment opportunities, as an example.

"In Saskatchewan, 70 percent of what a person gets (on social assistance) goes to rent alone, on average...then there's only a couple of hundred bucks left over and people are really scrambling," he says.

The physician and advocate urged the crowd to consider that health and wellbeing is "the best measure of how we're doing as a society." If we don't spend money on prevention and maintenance, he points out, then society as a whole suffers.

Meili, who was named Saskatoon's Global Citizen of the Year by the Saskatchewan Council for International Cooperation, nearly won the leadership of the Saskatchewan NDP in 2013, losing by only 44 votes.

Ottawa man says a basic income would have changed the trajectory of his life

June 26, 2015

By Roderick Benns

From the time he was a toddler, John Dunn was bounced around 13 times from one Ontario foster home to the next until he turned 18. He was originally taken into care due to complications from his mother's severe — and often suicidal — bi-polar disorder and alcoholism, and was separated from his three siblings in the process.

There was often abuse, and he knows the experiences left an imprint on the shape of his life.

"I think I began to develop a constant mourning...of friends, family, and pretty well anything I began to become familiar with," Dunn, now 44, tells *Leaders and Legacies*.

His foster home experiences "had devastating effects on how I saw myself, my confidence, and how I deal with people and authority figures."

He didn't really appreciate what he had gone through until he finally had an emotional breakdown at the age of 32. He began to seek therapy to try and figure out what was wrong, "and why I could never hold a job more than a few months at a time without quitting or getting fired for making mistakes, forgetting things, getting overly frustrated, and hating himself for it."

He was soon diagnosed with post-traumatic stress disorder, having memory issues, and ADHD.
When he left foster care at age 18, Dunn thought he was free. He didn't realize that what he considered freedom would simply

become a web of precarious work and poverty traps that he has spent a lifetime trying to free himself from. He soon realized, instead, that he had no support at all to help him transition into a life.

"I was alone, and very, very broken."

Life on Social Assistance

Dunn thought about going to university but felt intimidated by even walking into the building, "let alone figuring out where I was ever going to get the money to pay for it." He says he didn't know about school loans back then and just figured he couldn't go because he didn't have any family to help.

The Ottawa man admits he has had a checkered employment past due to his life experiences. He has done everything from factory work, to video editing, to working as a messenger. He even worked a year at CBC as a tech support. However, he doesn't consider himself to have any particular area of expertise, "since, like my childhood, I never seemed to be able to stay anywhere for any length of time."

For the last year, he has been living on social assistance in Ottawa, the city he has called home for more than a decade. It isn't enough to live on, says Dunn, and he points out that he doesn't smoke and has never gotten into drugs. He also gave up drinking nearly two years ago.

The Ottawa man says he gets approximately $625 a month in total through social assistance. His monthly budget is as follows:

- Rent: $400 for a basement room
- Bus Pass: $100
- Groceries: $60
- Phone: $40
- Entertainment: $25 (coffee shops, etc.)

"Right now, I typically run out of groceries by mid-month," Dunn says. When he gets too hungry, he knows he will have to start "the degrading process of asking others for food or a couple of dollars here and there."

E-book initiative

To try and earn a little more money and to be of service to others, Dunn has been writing a 'For Regular People' series of e-books. The first book is *Reading and Understanding Canadian Legislation* and it walks the reader through the basics of how to read legislation by describing its basic elements.

The second book in the series he is currently writing is *Advocacy and Change Using Canadian Legislation* which will document actual examples of advocacy which have already been done to help people in various situations based on, or while using, legislation as their core guides.

Dunn, who is motivated to write these based on his own experiences with the system, also created a documentary for CBC Radio in 2002 called "Too Many Stops," in which he takes the listener on a virtual subway ride through life in foster care.

Life with a Basic Income Guarantee instead of welfare

A basic income guarantee – a policy that would ensure no person in Canada would ever fall below a set, annual income threshold — is currently being considered by policy makers and in jurisdictions across Canada. This includes the government of Prince Edward Island, the federal Liberal Party and Green Party, the mayors of Edmonton and Calgary, and high profile senators, among others.
While there are many types of basic income, many feel that a guaranteed annual income of $18,000 to $20,000 for individuals would be the threshold to keep people out of poverty.

When asked how a basic income guarantee from the government set at even $1,500 per month would change his life, Dunn was overwhelmed at the thought of this level of support.

"It would be a miracle in many ways. Not just financially, but emotionally and mentally," he says.

"I could also actually do some of the things many people take for granted, like maybe go out to a movie...or buy a coffee for a friend for once instead of always being the one who is treated."

Dunn says he would get some healthier food for his cat, who has been a friend and companion for 10 years. Then, thinking about himself, he adds "I could even get healthy food, too, instead of always the cheapest of the cheap which is not always" the best for people.

He says if he had to sum it up in a word, a basic income would give him a feeling of "dignity."

When asked how a basic income would change his day-to-day thinking, knowing it would prevent him from slipping into poverty, Dunn was enthusiastic about what that would mean.

"If I lose my work...because of accidents, or my own mistakes, or, in the case of abusive managers...and my post-traumatic reactions to them, I would not have to go into panic mode," he says.

He says it isn't a good feeling to think he is going to lose his basement room that he rents, or risk losing his pet cat.

"I would not have to go into the extreme stress I go into repeatedly when looking for work in a full-time mode all day long every day, getting rejection after rejection."

Since the entire welfare bureaucracy would be eliminated under almost any basic income guarantee model, Dunn notes he would no longer have to spend his time applying for welfare, "tying up their staff who are already overworked and have no time to deal effectively with all the clients they must process every day."

"I would be able to just keep my ears open for the right job at the right time as I find them, in a much more relaxed and natural way."

When asked what he might have done after leaving the foster care system at the age of 18, if a basic income guarantee had already been in place in Canada, Dunn says he definitely would have opened up a savings account to start.

"I may have seen a future in education. I may have decided to go to college or university because having some money allows for that type of thinking."

Once he put away some money, he figures he likely could have gotten a car.

"Which could also open up driving jobs, or other jobs which I might be able to do but are not within the reach of public transit," he explains.

Dunn says he would simply have had "more dignity and self-worth," if a basic income guarantee was there for him when he transitioned into adulthood. Everything always seemed as if it were for someone else, he says.

"So I never tried — and I never had anyone to support me or to give me pep talks. If only we could go back. Maybe I would have been a lawyer, a stock broker, a pilot, a financial adviser, a writer, a documentary producer — a person with dreams...and a means to accomplish those dreams."

"At the least, it would have meant the possibility to strive toward any one of these passions."

Basic income and healthy minimum wage go hand in hand, says retired professor

July 3, 2015

Roderick Benns recently interviewed Toni Pickard about basic income policy. Pickard was a law professor at Queen's University before she retired and is now the co-founder of the Kingston Action Group for a Basic Income Guarantee.

Benns: *We hear often that basic income could replace the need for higher minimum wages. Many point out that with the scarcity of jobs, a better minimum wage will only reach a minority of people anyway. What do you believe?*

Pickard: For me, minimum wages and basic income go together like bread and butter. Together they are wonderful. Each alone serves a purpose, but only one leaves a lot to be desired. Some recent media discussion seems premised on the view that the two are an either-or proposition. I don't see why. They have different conceptual bases, different beneficiaries and different payers. There's no need to choose between them.

Minimum wages are for those who have jobs, obviously. They're about decent pay for work, and an end to the false assumption that working people and their employers have equal bargaining power. That might be true for highly sought individuals at high salaried levels but it's not true for most of us. The wages are paid for by employers.

Basic income is for those without sufficient income to live decently, without regard to their job status and is paid collectively. At the very least, it's about an end to hunger, homelessness and other forms of destitution and alleviation from income insecurity in face of potential job loss. Basic income is paid for by all of us.

From self-interest, employers seeking profits want to keep wage rates as low as is consistent with getting the necessary work done. Our collective self-interest is to ensure basic income levels sufficient to lift people out of poverty and to provide an income floor for everyone else to arrest a free fall into poverty should financial calamity hit. Once these differences are understood clearly, it seems obvious to me why we need both.

Working together, the two will put an adequate income into the hands of all those who didn't before have enough to live decently. Together they provide the greatest nourishment for the economy. People living on low incomes need to spend all the money they have so the money paid out will continue to circulate in the economy (unlike the $684 billion of 'dead money said to be stored in corporate bank accounts, doing the economy no good whatsoever). And the money will be spent close to home, supporting local businesses, increasing local employment opportunities, building up local economies and increasing tax revenues.

It's true that the number of job holders is dwindling. Canada's rate of labour participation hit a 13 year low in December of 2014. It will almost certainly continue to drop given globalization, austerity policies and, most worrisome, rapidly developing technology which is affecting almost all job categories. I'm not at all sure, however, that the absolute number of minimum wage jobs is decreasing. For the moment, their proportion of all jobs is increasing. According to Stats Canada, almost half the 59,000 new jobs created in May 2015 were part-time jobs.

I know some people believe that if done properly and paid at adequate levels, basic income will obviate the need for minimum wage legislation. I think the idea is that individuals with an adequate basic income will no longer be forced to accept whatever job can be had in order to live. While that's true, I can't agree that therefore minimum wage legislation won't be needed.

First, even if smaller numbers of people will be working for minimum wages in the future, almost certainly there will be millions who still do. Happily, basic income will prevent hunger and homelessness, but basic is basic and not very satisfying. Most people able to work in the job market will want to improve their lives and prospects if possible. I don't believe that those who can find work will all have the wherewithal to stand up to employers by insisting on a decent wage. Nor are such people likely to be unionized. Without minimum wage legislation employers will be able to exploit vulnerable job seekers and then basic income, paid through taxes, will end up subsidizing private businesses.

I believe that taxpayers should not be called on to subsidize private businesses through provision of a basic income. Both a fair distribution of the cost of doing business and market efficiency are best served by having a legislated minimum wage as well. Fairness argues that those who profit personally and directly from the work of others, not the taxpayers at large, should pay the expenses of producing their profits. If owners who had been skimping on wages choose to close up shop in face of minimum wage legislation, that shouldn't be an economic concern. If market theory works at all, they'll be replaced by more efficient competitors.

To my mind, ending minimum wage laws leaves those most in need of the law's protection without it, valuing profit making over human well-being. That some basic income recipients might be willing to accept very low wages does not justify abandoning minimum wage protection for working people at large. Basic income is a good thing but it gets nowhere near equalizing bargaining power between job seekers and employers.

Benns: *Will a basic income shrink the pool of people willing to do work? Will it 'hollow out' our labour force, as some fear?*

Pickard: No, I don't believe it will be what's usually called a 'work disincentive.' That's a widespread concern, but the evidence from basic income trials of all kinds in many different places and in different time periods simply doesn't bear the prediction out. In the Dauphin experiment in Manitoba in the 1970s, the impact of basic income on primary wage earners was negligible. With respect to secondary and tertiary earners in a family, there was a small impact due to high school students completing their degrees rather than leaving to help support the family and, in a period before maternity leaves were commonplace, young mothers staying home longer with infants and young children.

A pilot in a very different culture and different historical period — within the last five years in India — showed even more positive results. Those receiving the income actually increased their paid labour participation and engaged in some entrepreneurial activities. Similar results can be found in almost all studies wherever and whenever the experiment has been tried. Since basic income provides relief from stress resulting in better health, more energy, time freed up from scrambling to make ends meet, etc., it's understandable that people who receive it are more able to work or start up small businesses. And since it furnishes what's basic only, it's understandable that people want to do what they can to improve their living standard.

But the more important point is that even if basic income were to 'hollow out' the labour force, that shouldn't worry anyone. We all know the labour market is shrinking. There won't be enough jobs for all the people who are willing and able to work. The real problem is what to do about the forces beyond our control. Even the Canadian government's power is limited. No government, no matter how creative and caring its policies, can stop the progress of globalization and automation. What's needed is for them all, federal, provincial and municipal, to take a clear-eyed look at the impact of those forces in order to find ways to buffer us against the damage they will continue to inflict.

Basic income isn't part of the problem, it's part of the solution.

Basic income would alleviate inequality, improve our health: former banker

July 14, 2015

By Roderick Benns

When his parents left Holland for Canada, Gary H. J. Pluim was just 13 years old. His father was in the furniture business in Holland, but he watched his dad struggle in his adopted homeland. At one point his father developed symptoms of depression. All eight kids did what they could do and the older ones, including Pluim, got part time jobs to help out financially.

His father told Pluim to go to the welfare office to ask for a loan.

"He didn't want to go on welfare, he just wanted the help a loan would give him," Pluim tells *Leaders and Legacies*.

They told the young Pluim that his father had to come in himself, and that they "don't do loans."

"I was laughed out of the office," Pluim says.

Eventually, his father got help from the local church with a loan, and Pluim says he never looked back. Pluim grew up and went on to a 30-year banking career, then switched gears and worked for charities like World Vision and WaterCan (now WaterAid) for 22 years after that.

When he thinks back to those early days in Canada, Pluim can't help but think that a basic income guarantee policy would have really helped his family.

"I saw my father struggling, through no fault of his own. Many people get into situations through no thought of their own. Sometimes it's mental health. Sometimes it's other things."

Pluim, an Ottawa resident, saw former Conservative Senator Hugh Segal about a year and a half ago on television, speaking about a basic income guarantee (also known as a negative income tax or a guaranteed annual income.) He was fascinated as Segal walked through the advantages of the policy, which typically means ensuring a person would never fall below a set threshold of income. The idea is to keep everyone above the poverty line – to have their basic needs met.

Pluim also felt disturbed to realize how much inequality has been growing in Canada over many years. The richest one per cent of Canadians took almost a third of all income gains from 1997 to 2007—the decade with the fastest-growing incomes in this generation, according to a 2010 study by Armine Yalnizyan.

"I was fascinated by what he (Segal) had to say, and it never left my mind. I would chat with others about it because it interested me so much."

Now, Pluim is seeing an increasing amount of discussion about a basic income guarantee happen across Canada and around the world. He's even seeing a family connection.

Dr. Lisa Simon, who led the successful push for all Ontario health units to support basic income policy, is Pluim's daughter-in-law. In the resolution from the Association of Local Public Health Agencies (alPHa) that she helped author, the association defined a basic income guarantee as a "cash transfer from government to citizens not tied to labour market participation," enough to ensure "everyone an income sufficient to meet basic needs and live with dignity, regardless of work status..."

The resolution also points out that basic income "resembles income guarantees currently provided in Canada for seniors and children, which have contributed to health improvements in those age groups."

Leaner bureaucracy, better health

As someone who worked in the financial services industry for most of his life, Pluim says he was first drawn to appreciating the idea of basic income as an "opportunity to eliminate a lot of bureaucracy." Under almost all basic income models, at least welfare systems would be dismantled.

"If we can make this policy happen through the income tax return system it would be very efficient," says Pluim, who believes strongly in free enterprise and entrepreneurialism.

Now, from the work that Dr. Simon has shared with him and from his subsequent reading, Pluim also recognizes the health benefits when there is financial stability in families' lives. He adds there has to be "incentives built in" for people to work, but he also doesn't believe that will be a problem, pointing out that when people lose their job due to downsizing, they don't stop looking for work just because they know Employment Insurance is coming.

"I think people want to work. I think people are hardwired to contribute."

Pluim wants to urge politicians of all stripes to have a national discussion about a basic income guarantee policy.

"Someone needs to drive this. I really believe this generation can make the changes we need to make our society fairer."

Lived poverty experience: Kingston woman wonders what basic income would have meant for her family

July 24, 2015

Roderick Benns recently interviewed Tanya Beattie, a public health promoter with Kingston, Frontenac and Lennox and Addington Public Health. In this wide ranging interview, Beattie discusses her own lived experience with poverty, the social determinants of health, and a basic income guarantee policy.

Benns: *You have had lived poverty experience – can you talk a little about your background? Where did you grow up? What are some key experiences from your childhood that stayed with you?*

Beattie: Yes, I was born, educated, and now work in Kingston, Ontario. I spent much of my growing up years living in the north end, which is known as Rideau Heights here, with my mother and periodically also with her family. We moved around a fair bit. My family did not have much and struggled on a day-to-day basis to provide the basics. This left a distinct impression on me and my development and how I viewed — and continue to view — the world.

Specifically, I seemed to understand from a young age that my life was not normal, that it wasn't normal to not have food in the house, to spend so much time on my own even as a very young child, to know that alcohol could change people and their choices about what was important — that even those who were supposed to protect and care for you could be incapable of actually doing so.

I saw the struggle, even though I couldn't possibly understand the details or the impacts it had on the emotional and physical well-being of my family. But I knew it was wrong. This knowledge, however, couldn't protect me from the developmental trauma I experienced as a child living in very adverse conditions for healthy development. I was very lucky to have had such positive experiences at school. I was a good student, was liked by my teachers and was able to make lots of friends. School was my real home, my safe place, a family that supported and encouraged me to try and made me believe I could do anything. Without it I can honestly say I have no idea what would have happened to me, I doubt I would have been anywhere near as successful in making a life of my own.

Benns: *How did these experiences shape who you became?*

Beattie: These experiences left a tremendous void in my development. Trauma I experienced has made my life challenging in ways that I am only now beginning to understand. It has also made it possible for me to see the world through a very different lens. Where others spend decades developing an understanding of how living conditions truly impact lives, with some never actually being able to comprehend or empathize, I came by this through my lived experiences.

Some may call this anecdotal evidence, and they would be right. But sometimes anecdotal evidence proves to be no less accurate than highly rigorous research studies — which in the case of the social determinants of health at first feels anecdotal, or perhaps even obvious, but yet too big to do anything about it. We now know that living in adverse conditions has negative and long lasting effects on us. Particularly children, but adults as well will suffer poor physical and mental health outcomes when their basic needs and ability to participate in society are limited. A study in the US that looked at adverse childhood experiences really demonstrates how health outcomes are impacted by living experiences and the more adverse they are, the more likely it is that individuals will suffer in the future.

All of this has made me into a person who wants to help make things better. I also see the possible reasons why people do the things they do — even the hurtful 'bad' things. So I try particularly hard not to judge others, even those who have done me harm personally. I do not blame them, even though I do feel anger about it. I recently heard a very accurate statement — hurt people hurt people. It is a logical and natural consequence that makes it impossible for me to place blame on anyone, aside from perhaps those who work directly to create the legislation and public policies that build the foundations for society.

Benns: You're a public health promoter in Kingston now. Did you make a conscious choice to go into this field because of your own upbringing? Do you ever see echoes of your own childhood experiences in the people you meet?

Beattie: Interestingly I did not make a conscious choice to end up working in this area, but when I look back at the path that I took it would seem like there was some kind of unconscious plan being followed. I have been working in public health for almost 13 years, specifically in the area of reducing harms and deaths related to alcohol use. I see reflections of my own childhood experiences, but not always directly, as the majority of my time is spent at a desk. Yet in the research and strategies I help develop, and in everything I do I try to maintain a sense of the real world and what types of roles, influences and struggles people must go through when making decisions.

It is never so simple as an individual's personal responsibility. I bring my understanding of the struggles individuals face when trying to achieve success in life. This often means healthy choices are not often a direct priority. Working with the community to help work on what individuals need is always where I start from.

Benns: *How would a basic income guarantee policy have changed life for your family, when you were growing up? What different decisions may have been taken? What different paths may have been chosen?*

Beattie: A basic income guarantee would have changed a lot of things for my life. My parents wouldn't have had to struggle for our very basic needs; maybe they wouldn't have divorced; maybe I wouldn't have been exposed to traumatizing violent events; maybe I would have had a stable, safe and secure home with healthy and nutritious food; maybe my parents wouldn't have had to choose between working and leaving me alone by myself when I was far too young to be left alone.

Or, perhaps my mother and father would have separated from one another sooner had they had the income to support themselves individually, which would have decreased the violence and awfulness to which we were all exposed. So many pleasant possibilities. It's difficult to gauge where we all would have ended up, had we each had the benefit of a basic income guarantee, but I am sure our opportunities in life were diminished without it.

Benns: *Why do you fight for a basic income guarantee policy today?*

Beattie: I have been working for most of my life in one way or another to help make the world a better, safer and more equitable place. There is so much to do, so many ways to contribute time to this, that as most people eventually figure out, one must focus energies in one area. So I have ended up choosing to focus on basic income because I see it as the best way to effect the biggest change for the most people. I am a two-birds-with-one-stone kind of person, and a basic income would hit many birds so to speak — it would give people the means to meet their individual needs while maintaining dignity and respect. This doesn't mean that other important public policies that will improve the social determinants of health, such as the living wage movement, should be ignored of course, and I am glad there are others working on this as well.

Financial stability, formal education, would have changed woman's life path

July 27, 2015

By Roderick Benns

Living in poverty in northeastern New Brunswick wasn't the hardest thing Maggie Olscamp had to experience while growing up in the 1950s — it was watching her father leave home to find work out of province to help support them.

Her father — an artist, draughtsman, and cartographer — sometimes found work in Goose Bay, Labrador, or Tilt Cove in Newfoundland. Sometimes it was among the Inuit in Canada's far north. It wasn't the fact of poverty itself, but rather consequences like this that left its real mark.

"Poverty is relative. There were always some who were worse off than we were," Olscamp, now 69, says. "The hardest thing was seeing my father having to go away to find work."

As a young girl of about eight or nine, Olscamp recalls she told her grandmother that she was going to be an artist when she grew up. Years later, a first place win in the Canada-wide Canadian Forestry Association Forest Fire prevention contest anchored this belief further, when she was 14.

In Grade 10, Olscamp entered her high school's 'industrial program.' All she really wanted was the drafting program, but she was also exposed to electrical, machine shop, and motor mechanics.

"Up to that time, no female had been allowed into the industrial program in any Canadian school. My drawings, plus the fact that the department head respected my father's work, convinced them to let me in."

She spent her summer studying books they used in the department. Boys had been taking industrial arts since Grade 7, "and I had...a lot of catching up to do," she says.

Olscamp recalls that in the fall her marks were the highest in the class and all the boys in the class treated her with respect. But she had to leave school in the middle of Grade 10 for personal reasons — partly to do with a teacher and partly because her mother was ill and needed help at home.

"I believe I would eventually have become an architect had things been different back then," she reflects.

With her high school education interrupted, this stunted her college and university path early on. Throughout her life she would hold a myriad of odd jobs and positions in both New Brunswick, Ontario, and the United States. Such jobs included being a waitress, bookkeeper, seamstress, retail clerk, and helping with her husband's business, among many others. This was always in addition to working on her art career on the side, which remains a constant companion.

Although she later attended university as a mature student, financial and family circumstances always seem to conspire against finishing her course work. She got married and had two children and says that "during all the years of struggle to be financially independent and to build a career" for herself, she tried to be "the best mother I could to my two children."

"That they have grown into exceptional people is my greatest joy."

Olscamp believes that part of the consequences of her life's directional arc is that she now lives on less than $10,000 per year. Her partner receives a little bit more. They live along Chaleur Bay in northeastern New Brunswick, an area she believes has been forgotten by most, once there was no longer a pressing need for the natural resources that fed hungry government coffers for most of a century.

"As long as our mines and mill were operating, at least some of my fellow citizens had good jobs," she tells *Leaders and Legacies*. "Some were able to travel away to get a decent education. Some were not."

A Basic Income Guarantee

Olscamp wonders if a basic income guarantee policy had existed how it might have changed things, both for her family and herself. While there are many models of how to set up a basic income policy, many feel that a guaranteed annual income of $18,000 to $20,000 for individuals would be the threshold to keep people out of poverty.

"Financial independence would definitely have led me down a different path. I would have been able to afford a formal education...I would certainly have lived my life as a respected professional instead of being regarded as a high-school dropout who never held down a steady job," she says.

Today, she and her partner share a modest house on the edge of town and one car. She restricts herself to going into town only three days a week to work in her downtown art studio, which is open to the public.

"It is an old building in need of repair and much too costly to heat in winter — otherwise I might move there."

Her income derived from her art in her lifetime would be very modest, she says, and that "what I've sold over the years would not come close to what I have spent in material and supplies."

Nonetheless, her studio is "pretty well the extent of my social life," Olscamp says. "If I could afford taxis I would participate in community cultural events. I try not to complain too much about this because I know I'm not the only senior who lives such an existence. Many others have tried to convince themselves that Facebook is a substitute for real human contact but I don't think so."

Olscamp says she is certain that she "would have fared much better" in life if she had received some sort of basic Income that she could have called her own. She believes each individual person should receive the same basic income and then let Revenue Canada make adjustments.

"Revenue Canada can iron out who gets to keep their cheque and who gets clawed back."

When asked how a basic income guarantee from the government set at $1500 per month ($18,000 per year) might change her life, Olscamp says that she would have "fewer concerns and more choices."

She notes that, among other things, she would:

- not be worried about bills not being paid
- invest in solar heating to avoid wood use during winter
- pay off the mortgage
- eat better
- give graduation gifts to her two grandkids
- see a dentist
- get new glasses every couple of years
- go to an opera, ballet, orchestra, or see a play occasionally
- travel to participate in art and music workshops
- move closer to downtown Bathurst
- outfit a studio where she could hold art/music events

Olscamp says she has never been in a situation where she felt financially secure and independent, throughout her years of child-rearing, followed by years of chronic unemployment.

"I speak from long experience when I say that a basic income for every citizen should be a basic human right."

Charlottetown mayor calls for basic income in tandem with other social supports

August 5, 2015

By Roderick Benns

It's time to improve the quality of life for all Canadians, says Charlottetown Mayor Clifford Lee — and the best way to do it is to implement a basic income guarantee policy.

Lee says such a policy – also known as a guaranteed annual income or minimum income — must be created in tandem with other social supports to be effective.

"I support the concept of a basic income guarantee, but a national discussion is needed to address affordable housing, addictions and available treatments, poverty and, as part of that, the idea of a basic income guarantee," he says.

Lee says with such a long federal election going on, "there's all kinds of time" to talk about poverty and issues like basic income policy, although he's not convinced that party leaders will yet.

Lee was one of the Canadian mayors invited to complete a national survey by *Leaders and Legacies*, in order to gauge municipal level support for a basic income. Support for basic income comes from many Canadian leaders, including Calgary Mayor Naheed Nenshi, who called for "brave steps" in the fight against inequality. Nenshi vowed to connect with other Canadian mayors to push for a basic income guarantee.

As well, Edmonton Mayor Don Iveson says the "evidence is overwhelming" for providing a basic income guarantee to Canadians. At the provincial level, in Prince Edward Island, Premier Wade

MacLauchlan committed to basic income policy during the recent election campaign.

A common definition of a basic income guarantee ensures everyone an income sufficient to meet basic needs and live with dignity, regardless of work status. It involves a regular, reliable distribution of money from government to people to help ensure total income sufficient to meet common, basic needs.

Lee tells *Leaders and Legacies* that "until this country's leadership is able to sit down and address the quality of life issues that hold us back, then Canada will not become what it should be."

He says for too long the three levels of government "have drawn lines in the sand" about whose responsibility it is to tackle various social issues, including poverty, and the result of this posturing has slowed progress. As well, tax revenue sharing is a significant issue that needs to be addressed for all cities, he says, because it's not acceptable for municipalities to continue to raise taxes.

While he acknowledges the City of Charlottetown is not responsible for social services (unlike some other municipalities in other parts of Canada), he says the principled thing to do when holding an elected office is to advocate on behalf of citizens' needs.

"There's no question that as elected officials we have a responsibility to address ongoing issues" that we see in our communities, he says, "beyond snow removal" and other basic services. He says this is one of the reasons he is speaking out about a basic income guarantee policy and other social issues.

Lee says he is not looking to blame other levels of government. However, he says that leaders from all three levels of government should realize it's "only going to be a matter of time" before Canadians demand elected officials address this."

The mayor notes that from a social angle, Charlottetown is focusing on family violence prevention and affordable housing. An affordable housing summit that was held last fall to look into the housing needs of city residents was sidelined with elections. Lee says he will be "reactivating" this group by the end of the year to continue their work.

When asked if work incentives needed to be built into a basic income guarantee policy, Lee notes that he doesn't believe this will be an issue.

"I honestly believe that Charlottetonians, Prince Edward Islanders, and all Canadians sincerely want to contribute to their society."

Referring to basic income policy, he says that "if we create a vehicle to allow them to play that role, we'll succeed."

Canada is looking to Prince Edward Island for leadership on basic income guarantee policy

August 7, 2015

By Roderick Benns

Perhaps now, in the middle of a federal election, it would be a good time to stop pretending that we are helpless to eliminate poverty. In a nation as wealthy and as privileged as Canada, poverty is simply a social construction. It is the result of decisions we continue to make (or not make) as a society — and it is costing us dearly. Inequality breeds poorer health outcomes. It drains our economy. It compromises our moral purpose as one of the world's leading nations.

Calgary Mayor Naheed Nenshi and Edmonton Mayor Don Iveson galvanized discussion on this issue earlier this spring when they spoke out strongly in favour of a basic income policy. Their comments to *Leaders and Legacies* were picked up and shared across Canada.

Leaders and Legacies, in turn, decided to launch a national survey of Canadian mayors to gauge municipal support for basic income policy. Charlottetown Mayor Clifford Lee was one of the first municipal leaders to respond to this survey, indicating his support for basic income. Lee believes it would be most effective if it was implemented in tandem with other social supports, such as affordable housing and support for addictions.

A common definition of a basic income guarantee ensures everyone an income sufficient to meet basic needs and live with dignity, regardless of work status. It involves a regular, reliable distribution of money from government to people to help ensure total income sufficient to meet common, basic needs.

Lee says that "until this country's leadership is able to sit down and address the quality of life issues that hold us back, then Canada will not become what it should be."

We couldn't agree more — and Prince Edward Island seems to be leading the way. With all-party commitment to basic income guarantee policy, at least at some level, during the last provincial election, PEI is far ahead of any other province in its support. Premier Wade MacLauchlan's recent win means that all eyes are now on PEI to watch how this commitment will unfold.

The biggest elephant in the room is the fear that a large cross-section of people will simply stop being productive if they have a basic income. But there is ample evidence to suggest a basic income policy will not do this, from experiments done in Dauphin, Manitoba in the 1970s, Brazil in 2004 (and ongoing), a two-year pilot in Namibia from 2008-2010, and India in 2011.

Speaking about the most recent India experiment, renowned economist Guy Standing said that people worked more, not less, when their basic needs were met.

Charlottetown's mayor believes all Canadians "sincerely want to contribute to their society."

We agree and would like PEI — the birthplace of Canada — to take action now. This would spark a national conversation that could truly be a transformative step for our country. In this most fortunate of nations we already have the money and the basic income solution to eradicate poverty. The only question we must ask ourselves is how we feel about the fact that we haven't yet chosen to do it.

— *Roderick Benns is the publisher of Leaders and Legacies. This article was originally published in The Charlottetown Guardian.*

Manitoba mayor agrees with basic income policy, but only with work incentives

August 10, 2015

By Roderick Benns

As mayors across Canada are asked to comment on a basic income guarantee policy, Winkler, Manitoba Mayor Martin Harder is offering qualified support for such a policy.

Harder took part in a national survey conducted by *Leaders and Legacies*. He was one of the Canadian mayors who was contacted to gauge municipal support for basic income policy.

His city, Winkler, is about 100 kilometres southwest of Winnipeg. It's a growing hub of about 11,000 and is largely Mennonite.

"I believe that everyone has the right to a basic standard of living," Harder tells *Leaders and Legacies*, "but what I have an issue with is people not having any initiative" for themselves.

A common definition of a basic income guarantee ensures everyone an income sufficient to meet basic needs and live with dignity, regardless of work status. It involves a regular, reliable distribution of money from government to people to help ensure total income sufficient to meet common, basic needs.

Recognizing that welfare is not working well either, and that it acts as a work disincentive, Harder says balance is needed between a system that might breed mediocrity (basic income) and another one that could be overly capitalistic (a society with no safety nets.)

"I've had a life afforded to me that has been filled with opportunities, but those opportunities were not on the backs of others," he says, suggesting an overly-generous basic income program might be counterproductive to society from a work ethic angle.

"We don't want to create a complacent lifestyle," he adds.

However, experiments done in Dauphin, Manitoba in the 1970s, Brazil in 2004 (and ongoing), a two-year pilot in Namibia from 2008-2010, and India in 2011, among other examples, may suggest otherwise. Speaking about the most recent India experiment, renowned economist Guy Standing said that people worked more, not less, when their basic needs were met.

Despite what he calls the "danger of safety nets" Harder says a basic income policy might work if there was sufficient incentive for people to work.

"You don't want to make it so comfortable that there's no desire to better yourself," he says.

Alberta entrepreneur says basic income would allow people to contribute more

August 11, 2015

By Roderick Benns

Working hard to grow a business isn't easy, says Edmonton-area entrepreneur Chantelle Scott, but a basic income policy would make life a little less stressful in the first few challenging years.

Scott, inspired by Edmonton Mayor Don Iveson's support for basic income, is realizing how beneficial such a social policy would be for those people who are trying to carve out a job for themselves.

"Many people assume that if someone owns a small business, they are doing quite well for themselves," she says. "They don't realize that every cent you had went into the creation of that store."

A common definition of a basic income guarantee ensures everyone an income sufficient to meet basic needs and live with dignity, regardless of work status. It involves a regular, reliable distribution of money from government to people to help ensure total income sufficient to meet common, basic needs.

Scott owns Nevaeh, a retail store in the hamlet of Sherwood Park, on the east side of Edmonton. The store is focused on spiritual supplies for all faiths, such as healing stones, herbs for incenses, teas, and rubs. She also does local consignment for other Sherwood Park entrepreneurs so they too, have an opportunity to sell product within a store front.

Two years ago, Scott was still working for a video duplication and editing company field, where she had been for 10 years. When the company lost its largest contract, she was told her job was going to be eliminated. She looked for many jobs, both in her area of expertise and in connected fields, but had no luck. With her passion for new age spiritual dimensions, she launched Nevaeh, given there was no similar business in Sherwood Park.

"People say the first year is the hardest but that is not so," says Scott. "The first year, you have savings. Your credit is reasonable and if you are lucky you have Employment Insurance (EI) during the set up and promotion phase," she explains.

In year two, she notes, sales increase but the extra money is gone, so there is less replenishment of inventory when items sell. "The second year is the true struggle because you hit the dreaded stage of paying expenses on the credit line and the credit card."

Scott says she would have preferred to have been able to take some business courses and learn more before jumping into opening a store – but she couldn't afford to wait.

"There is pressure when you are on EI or Alberta Works, and there is fear. The programs inhibit job growth because you always know you will lose most of the support if you find a job, and if it is a bad job you are stuck," says Scott.

She notes there is no one or no place to help someone find the "right job," nor is there opportunity to rest after leaving a very stressful job.

"You have seven months to figure out your life and it starts immediately — but you also have six to eight weeks of no benefits, so you need to already use up your savings before anything has even begun."

Scott says that a basic income (also called a guaranteed annual income) would help entrepreneurs survive. A guaranteed income would allow me to pay bills, buy food and be able to pay down the start-up costs of the business, which would eventually allow me to be able to extend my hours sooner, attend more trade fairs and markets, and hire staff."

Scott says that many people believe that any form of guaranteed income will encourage laziness, or will put an end to small business.

"That is not the case. Guaranteed income allows people who cannot get jobs to create their own. It allows disabled people who are unable to get pensions to do home-based businesses and still survive. It allows single people who do not benefit from child tax credits or pension splitting to have enough money for food and essentials...to afford a better life," she says.

Scott says that if people have a guaranteed income, then they will choose to spend more. "They have a higher standard of living, they eat better, and they are healthier both physically and mentally."

While acknowledging that some may take advantage of such a social program, she says she has to believe that "the tip of the iceberg" would be more like her own story. "Average, normal, educated people who have trouble gaining employment, not because they have no education or work ethic," but for more intangible reasons, like competition, or too much or too little experience.

If an entrepreneur is given the opportunity to survive early on, it is not only a boon to them, but to the larger economy, she says.

"A guaranteed income policy would allow so many to live their dreams and to truly contribute to society."

Sarnia mayor frustrated with federal leaders for ignoring poverty, inequality

August 19, 2015

By Roderick Benns

One of Canada's longest serving mayors is getting frustrated with the three main federal party leaders who are persistently ignoring the issues of poverty and inequality.

Mayor Mike Bradley, of Sarnia, Ontario, says he is speaking out more lately for measures to deal with inequality – such as a basic income guarantee policy – "because others don't."

All three main political parties are constantly referencing the middle class, he says, at the expense of all others. (In fact, in the last debate, only Green Party leader Elizabeth May mentioned inequality and suggested the issue needed far more attention.)

Mayor Bradley says the people that need a voice are the ones who are struggling.

"They don't have the energy and the time. They need someone to advocate for them. That's why I think it's important to speak out, because inequality continues to grow."

Bradley was one of many mayors from across Canada contacted by *Leaders and Legacies* for a national survey to gauge municipal support for basic income policy.

A common definition of a basic income guarantee ensures everyone an income sufficient to meet basic needs and live with dignity, regardless of work status. It involves a regular, reliable distribution of money from government to people to help ensure total income sufficient to meet common, basic needs.

Bradley says Sarnia – a city of about 72,000 on the Ontario-Michigan border — is not the only community that could benefit from a basic income guarantee policy.

"It doesn't matter the community — you see huge gaps in haves and have-nots, now, and its growing."

"Many of the social issues that develop are simply because people are struggling. They don't have the ability to deal with their essential needs. This is a country of incredible wealth and we can't even meet the basic needs of our populations," he says.

Circle Program

The mayor says it's a problem when people try to simplify the solutions to poverty, because it's never one issue. From homelessness, addictions, mental health issues, education, and transportation and employment, everything needs to be considered, he says.

A program that Lambton County adopted called Circles has been a game changer on the ground, he says, and it's something the municipality is proud of. According to their website, Circles is a "supportive, intentional, reciprocal, befriending relationship comprised of a Circle Leader, a family working to get out of poverty, and two to four community Allies — middle class people who are willing to befriend the family and support their way out of poverty."

The Circles Campaign:

- Builds intentional relationships across class and race lines
- Identifies barriers that keep people in poverty
- Implements innovative solutions

- Creates partnerships to help families
- Changes the goals of the system to support families

Bradley says community members with various skills come together to support people who are on social assistance, with about 50 families involved so far. The program is so successful it is being adopted by other communities. He points out that sometimes it's best not to wait for the Province or Federal government to come to the rescue.

Basic Income Guarantee Policy

Bradley says he remembers basic income policy being debated during the Pierre Trudeau-Robert Stanfield years in the 1970s. The needs are greater now, he says, and inequality has risen, which is why he supports the policy.

"Today, federal politicians wait until the public is so far ahead of them and then they work to catch up. That's why I feel like it's part of my responsibility to raise these issues."

The mayor notes that social services offers no incentives to better oneself at all, and it just encourages an underground economy.

"It's a system structured for failure."

Bradley says that a single male on social assistance gets less than $600 a month, and it "defies common sense that he can survive."

The mayor says there will always be excuses governments can make for not dealing with inequality, but the fact remains a country as wealthy as Canada can always make the choice to implement a policy like a basic income.

"There's never a right time to do something — so let's just do it."

Quebec mayor says basic income would help young adults complete their education

August 24, 2015

By Roderick Benns

The mayor of Salaberry-de-Valleyfield, a city of 40,000 on the south shore of Montreal, says a basic income policy would help youth who have dropped out of high school to complete their education.

Mayor Denis Lapointe, who has been a 20-year veteran of municipal politics as mayor of the city, says his municipality has a fairly significant high school dropout rate, although many young people eventually try to access school and training.

"That (basic income) policy would help a fair percentage of unemployed people. It's not that there aren't any jobs — the problem is we have many young people who have not finished school" to be qualified for them, he says.

"Many people have left school before they've completed their education, and so to help get people back to school and training," a basic income policy could help bridge this, Lapointe explains.

Lapointe was one of many Canadian mayors who were invited to complete a national survey by *Leaders and Legacies*, in order to gauge municipal level support for a basic income guarantee policy.

Lapointe started his political career in 1995 when he was elected mayor of Salaberry-de-Valleyfield. He also sits as chairman on the board of directors of the Quebec Municipalities Union. Since 2005, he has been chairman of the Quebec Network of Healthy Cities and Towns.

The mayor says that each year, "young adults aged 22-23 are deciding after working for a while at a low salary they could go further" in life by improving their skills and finding better jobs.

"Every year we see an increase in adult education," he says, and he is concerned about poverty for young adults as they try to improve their skills.

Quebec municipalities unions talk basic income

Lapointe says in the coming weeks that both organizations representing all municipalities in the province will be discussing basic income. This includes the Union of Quebec Municipalities (UMQ) and Fédération québécoise des municipalités (FMQ).

"It's on the agenda. And for sure the message is going to be about the needs and expectations of communities," which will include measures for poverty reduction, he says.

The federal election and advocacy

The mayor says this federal election has been disappointing to him so far for what is — and what is not — being talked about. For instance, he is tired of hearing about Senator Mike Duffy and the related scandal involving Senate expenditures.

"There's nothing about social programs, nothing about people, nothing about fair salaries. It's a poor campaign," says LaPointe.

He says that political parties "want to be close to the middle class" but that "there's nothing for anyone else."

"What about our standard of living — what about everyone having a better life?" he asks.

Lapointe says citizens can put pressure on their elected representatives to advocate for measures like basic income. He points out there are also unions and community associations to join. Many associations work on poverty problems, he says, such as food security issues.

"These organizations are involved in bringing more equity into the social life of a community."

The mayor says citizens must speak louder and "bring their message to people like us — representatives of the city and the national politicians."

"It's time to do it while representatives are active from all the parties, because of the election," Lapointe says.

Reliable, basic income would lead to better self-worth, better life: Thunder Bay mayor

August 25, 2015

By Roderick Benns

Having a reliable income creates stronger self-worth and leads to a better life, says Mayor Keith Hobbs of Thunder Bay.

That's why the mayor supports a basic income guarantee policy, to help stem the tide of poverty, addiction, and homelessness that is afflicting too many Thunder Bay residents.

Hobbs was one of many Canadian mayors who were invited to complete a national survey by *Leaders and Legacies*, in order to gauge municipal level support for a basic income guarantee policy.

"If you have a basic income, you have a certain degree of self-worth. A set income and a 'housing first' strategy would work wonders," he says.

About 17,000 people live in low-income situations in Thunder Bay, the mayor says, and "a basic income would help with their needs."

Housing First

Just as important as basic income is being housed, according to the mayor.

"Homelessness is a big issue in Thunder Bay," says the mayor, and they want to move to a 'Housing First' model as soon as possible.

Housing first is an approach to ending homelessness that centres on quickly moving people who are homeless into independent, permanent housing. Additional supports and services are then provided as needed. The underlying thinking is that people can more easily move forward with a stable foundation — and studies show this is less expensive than constantly dealing with the social costs of homelessness.

The mayor is looking at both Edmonton and Medicine Hat, two Alberta cities, to find answers to his city's homelessness issue. In Medicine Hat, for example, between 2009 and 2015, 885 homeless people were housed. Medicine Hat's goal is to get people housed within 10 days of knowing they are homeless.

The catch, according to Hobbs, is that the Alberta city is funded at a much higher level by its province than Thunder Bay is. "All things being equal, we get very little from the Province and nothing from the Feds, who are getting out of housing supports."

The mayor says he does walk-abouts in his city, a picturesque centre of 122,000 on the north shore of Lake Superior, and he knows there are severe social issues. He points out that Thunder Bay has a significant indigenous population. People who leave their reserves from farther north end up in Thunder Bay, the largest urban area in northwestern Ontario. Once they leave their reserve, says the mayor, the federal government will no longer assist them. There are no immediate social safety nets to draw upon, he explains.

One of the city's most widely admired programs is Shelter House, which was acknowledged to be highly effective in a study completed by the University of Victoria. The program helps 15 of the most marginalized people to be taken off the streets. Their addictions are treated and they are housed until they are ready to move on.

"They are not being arrested or taking up a hospital bed. This project is working and we're going to keep funding as much as we can — and pitching it to the Province to fund," so that more than 15 people at a time can be assisted, he says.

Where is the leadership?

Hobbs says people are starving for leadership on the question of how municipalities are supposed to cope with the depth of social challenges they are facing.

"The current (Conservative) party is not helping. The federal Liberals before them didn't either," he says.

While he acknowledges the premier of Ontario, Kathleen Wynne, said she's committed to eradicating homelessness, it's "not good enough" until we see action.

"Municipalities are left carrying the bag."

Hobbs says citizens need to bring these issues of poverty reduction and basic income policy to the attention of federal level candidates and to the Province.

"People are acting apathetic. Talk to service groups. Talk to unions. Be vocal — election time is a great time for people to speak out."

For his part, Mayor Hobbs says he will be "looking at parties and candidates who are going to help fix these issues."

Ajax mayor says basic income policy the best way to conquer poverty

August 28, 2015

By Roderick Benns

A Greater Toronto Area mayor says Canada has the ability to eliminate poverty if the political will is there – and his gut tells him that a basic income guarantee is the way to do it.

Ajax Mayor Steve Parish was one of many Canadian mayors who were invited to complete a national survey by *Leaders and Legacies*, in order to gauge municipal level support for a basic income guarantee policy. The town – known for its 7 km of protected walking trails along Lake Ontario — is a centre of 110,000, about 25 kilometres east of Toronto.

"People who are chronically poor are not usually getting a good education, their health outcomes are not good, and...their needs are not being met. There is a moral cost but also a financial cost to society," for ignoring this truth, says Parish, who has been mayor for nearly 20 years.

Parish says he believes Canada has the ability "to provide enough income to keep people above the poverty level."

Ensuring Canadians have the basics to take care of their needs like food, shelter, and clothing is important, says the mayor, but also health care costs "not covered by our current system."

Parish says a basic income policy "would help break the cycle of poverty that is often passed on to generation to generation, in the same way that wealth is."

He knows that some people will immediately think about "a 38-year-old man avoiding work" when they think about a basic income guarantee.

"But they should be thinking about a million children across this country who have become imprisoned by poverty because their parents are. And that when they grow up, then chances are greater those children will grow up to face the same challenges. We can choose to break that cycle, though," the mayor says.

Pilot Projects

Parish says he believes setting up pilot projects ultimately makes sense, especially in smaller provinces where it might be quicker to set up a full program that can be studied for five to 10 years to collect hard data.

"We (politicians) are only going to get one chance to make a good first impression" with this policy, says the mayor, so having the data would be helpful.

"As a politician, I have to worry about these things because I know that's what opponents would latch on. I have to know about that 38 year old male who, yes, may not choose to work. But I also have to believe he would only represent" a tiny fraction of the whole.

"That's my gut instinct of what the reality is. Most people do not want to be unemployed. They want to move forward and they want their lives to be good ones. That's my basic view of humanity," says Parish.

"If the people demand it, then it's a matter of political will and priorities. Politicians will have their marching orders."

Five Newfoundland mayors endorse basic income policy

September 2, 2015

By Roderick Benns

Five Newfoundland mayors representing some of the largest centres on the island have endorsed basic income policy as a means of drastically reducing poverty.

St. John's mayor, Dennis O'Keefe, Corner Brook mayor, Charles Pender, Mount Pearl mayor, Randy Simms, Gander mayor, Claude Elliott, and Grand Falls-Windsor mayor, Al Hawkins have all agreed that "everyone in my city/community should be able to access a basic income guarantee."

The five leaders were among the Canadian mayors who were invited to complete a national survey by *Leaders and Legacies*, in order to gauge municipal level support for a basic income guarantee policy. Three other Newfoundland mayors are also anticipated to complete the survey – specifically, the mayors of Conception Bay South, Labrador City, and Paradise.

A common definition of a basic income guarantee ensures everyone an income sufficient to meet basic needs and live with dignity, regardless of work status. It involves a regular, reliable distribution of money from government to people to help ensure total income sufficient to meet common, basic needs.

Mayor O'Keefe, of St. John's, says in the survey that a basic income policy "is something all Canadians should support."

"It will be a tremendous help to many Canadians, men, women and children who live on the economic edge," he adds.

Mayor Simms of Mount Pearl notes that when governments are ready to set up a basic income policy, they should know "how it impacts the labour force and wage rates."

While acknowledging it would improve economic outcomes he is somewhat worried that it would reduce job opportunities and be de-motivating.

Grand Falls-Windsor Mayor Hawkins notes that "with an aging demographic, many of our seniors are facing serious financial challenges and are unable to meet their basic needs."

Hawkins says the policy would enable seniors to live without stress of meeting their financial obligations and give them some freedom to "do the things that they once enjoyed" but were prevented from because of a lack of income.

Leaders and Legacies continues to gather data from across Canada to track mayor-level support for basic income policy.

Local economies would benefit from basic income policy: Victoria mayor

September 7, 2015

By Roderick Benns

The mayor of Victoria, Lisa Helps, says basic income policy and robust local economies go hand in hand.

"There is a strong link between having a basic income and creating a strong local economy. There is more money to circulate and it supports the 'buy local' movement," she says.

"So that means it's good for the people who need more to live on, but also for the goods and services being sold by our business community," Helps says.

Helps is among a growing number of Canadian mayors who are speaking out about a basic income guarantee policy. Her city — Victoria — represents the third provincial capital leader to support the policy, along with Charlottetown, Prince Edward Island, and St. John's, Newfoundland.

A common definition of a basic income guarantee ensures everyone an income sufficient to meet basic needs and live with dignity, regardless of work status. It involves a regular, reliable distribution of money from government to people to help ensure total income sufficient to meet common, basic needs.

Helps says that out of the 13 municipalities that make up the Greater Victoria Area, with a population of 345,000, her city has the lowest average and median income in the region, at $38,000 a year.

"That's not affordable with the cost of housing and food," she says.

129

That's why Helps likes to talk about how to create prosperity for all, rather than 'combat poverty.' This re-framing is valuable, she says, because it serves to keep thinking about growth and improvement, rather than in a deficit model.

The Federal Election

Helps is hopeful that the federal party leaders will begin to address inequality issues more rigorously. She points out that the NDP have touched on important issues with their promise of a $15 universal child care program and the Liberals' promise of an enhanced Canada Child Tax Benefit is welcome news. The Green Party, she notes, has talked the most consistently about inequality — including a guaranteed liveable income.

"I don't think we can continue with the status quo in Canada. I want to see the rubber hit the road on these issues," she says.

Helps tells *Leaders and Legacies* that she already has her plane ticket booked for Ottawa in early December to petition the new government for action on basic income policy and other inequality issues, such as housing and homelessness. The federal election will be held October 19th.

Once she knows who the ministers are and what portfolios they hold, Helps says she will be on top of these issues for Victoria. She knows that mental health and addictions support, in addition to housing, would have to go hand in hand with a basic income guarantee.

Cities and Citizens Making a Difference

The mayor says she will continue to advocate and speak out about basic income and other issues that prevent economic prosperity for all people.

"I work to pass motions to the Federation of Canadian Municipalities. I focus on local economic development strategies. I also believe in creating social enterprises so that we can generate revenue and create a social good at the same time."

Helps says governments at all levels "need to pay attention to low income earners" because getting such earners more fully engaged in the economy benefits everyone. Citizens need to make noise, write letters, and pressure politicians, she says, to bring about the changes they want to see. At the same time, she believes it can only be effective "if elected officials are listening."

"The election is a great time to ask if there's any listening going on. We can point to the income inequality we are seeing in Canada. We can ask everyone what they're going to do about it. And we need to be very specific in our advocacy."

"We're working hard in the cities here and it would be nice to have a federal government that could help out," Helps says.

Mayor of Iqaluit says basic income would bring dignity to northern territory

September 11, 2015

By Roderick Benns

The mayor of Iqaluit, the capital of Nunavut, says basic income policy would bring dignity and equity to Canada's largest territory.

Mayor Mary Wilman says the multiple challenges of northern living on Baffin Island and in the rest of Nunavut are so great that citizens need basic income policy to lift them out of poverty.

"Due to a lack of roads and access, the only means of getting food here is through an annual shipping route and by air," says Wilman.

"That means we have to pay about three times as much for food as people pay in the south."

Minimum wage in Nunavut is $11 per hour – the same as Ontario. However, as the mayor points out, four litres of milk in Ontario is $3.99. In Iqaluit, it's $12. The average cost of 2.5 kilograms of flour in Nunavut is $13, and about $5 everywhere else in Canada.

"The minimum wage economy is based on southern living," she says.

According to the Globe and Mail, seven in 10 Inuit preschoolers in Nunavut live in homes without enough to eat. Median income for non-aboriginals in Nunavut is $86,600 a year; for the Inuit, it is $19,900. Eighty per cent of Nunavut's 36,585 people are Inuit and almost half the population is on social assistance.

"There's a lot of people up here who are unemployed," Wilman tells *Leaders and Legacies*.

She also points out that even old age pensioners often just get the bare minimum because there are few job opportunities where people could have had the chance to a pay into a pension.

"Therefore most live on the basic allotment from the government when they become of age — about $500 a month with no additional income."

Wilman is among a growing number of Canadian mayors who are pushing for higher levels of government to create a basic income guarantee policy.

She says she can "really see the good that basic income policy could do."

"It would bring dignity back to the people here. It could supplement other incomes," and improve education levels if people know they can go back to school without fear of being impoverished.

In a 2013 report prepared by the Caledon Institute of Social Policy, commissioned by Nunavut's Anti-Poverty Secretariat, the Institute recommended that Nunavut move to dismantle the welfare system and replace it with a basic income policy.

Wilman says many residents of Iqaluit want to become hunters to provide for their families, given there are few employment opportunities to choose from. The debate over the definition of what constitutes 'work' is clearly seen in Nunavut, where traditional ways of life are not recognized.

"Many people want to earn their own way, but people are struggling. If you're a full time traditional hunter, there's no extra income to can tap into. Traditional lifestyles up here are not recognized, so people end up becoming social assistance recipients."

People in the south often think becoming a hunter is practically free, she points out, but when you factor in the need for the right equipment, it can be quite costly to get set up. Transportation like a boat or a snowmobile is necessary, as is a weapon and ammunition, gas, and tools.

"All of this is needed to enable the hunter to become a viable contributor to the family."

Wilman sees basic income policy as a way of creating "social wellness."

"When you don't have the means to be independent it affects individuals' self-esteem. It's disheartening, not empowering. It's degrading."

The mayor says basic income policy was brought up again at a Baffin Island mayors' meeting last year. She points out that she is the only mayor in the territory lucky enough to be employed full time, because Iqaluit has city status. Almost all the other mayors in the territory are part time and could, in theory, also benefit from a policy like basic income.

"I advocate for my people here in Iqaluit, and in the other Nunavut communities," says Wilman. "We have talented, skillful people here who may not have the same opportunities to earn income like in other places in Canada."

Ten Ontario mayors speak out in favour of basic income policy

September 14, 2015

By Roderick Benns

Ten mayors from cities and towns across Ontario are speaking out in favour of basic income guarantee policy.

Many mayors across Canada were asked to complete a national survey by *Leaders and Legacies*, in order to gauge municipal level support for a basic income guarantee policy. Results are slowly being released as data is gathered. The mayors listed below have all indicated support for basic income policy at various levels:

Geoffrey Dawe – Aurora
Dan Mathieson – Stratford
Sandra Cooper – Collingwood
Nelson Santos – Kingsville
Gil Brocanier – Cobourg
Ted Luciani – Thorold
Aldo DiCarlo – Amherstburg
Gord Wauchope – Innisfil
John Henry – Oshawa
David Canfield — Kenora

A common definition of a basic income guarantee ensures everyone an income sufficient to meet basic needs and live with dignity, regardless of work status. It involves a regular, reliable distribution of money from government to people to help ensure total income sufficient to meet common, basic needs.

Mayor Nelson Santos of Kingsville says that a basic income guarantee policy would align well with his own town's municipal goals, even though he believes it is a "challenging initiative." However, he sees it as "very fitting for our region's poverty reduction strategy" in Windsor-Essex County.

In Cobourg, Mayor Gil Brocanier notes that it would allow his town to change its focus "from poverty reduction, homelessness, and affordable housing" to work on other social issues, given that income security for citizens would be more assured.

He also believes a basic income policy would help the business community by providing people "with more buying power."

Brocanier also sees some health benefits down the road, with better diets possible with more income. Students should also benefit, he believes, because they will be able to focus on their classroom learning without undue worry about poverty.

The Cobourg mayor cautions that any such guaranteed annual income policy would require upfront education for the public, since all benefits won't be immediately visible.

In Thorold, Ontario, Mayor Ted Luciani says the "income gap between rich and poor is increasing" every moment.

"We have to start closing this gap," he says, so "let's get it done."

Mayor Aldo DiCarlo of Amherstberg says he supports basic income policy, but not in isolation of also finding a way to create "higher paying, higher skilled job creation."

Kenora Mayor David Canfield adds that it's important to base a guaranteed annual income "on need and affordability" and to encourage people to improve their circumstances through working for a living wherever possible.

Montreal-area mayor says basic income needed to end poverty

September 17, 2015

By Roderick Benns

A Montreal-area mayor says it's time to adopt a basic income policy in Canada to eliminate poverty.

Mayor Danie Deschenes of Notre–Dame-de-l'Île-Perrot, just west of the island of Montreal in Quebec, says "all elected officials could be supporting the idea of all citizens having a basic income."

She sees it as a way to overcome poor housing and a sub-standard quality of life for people. "As elected officials, we should strive to improve our citizens' lives and the lives of their children," says Deschenes.

Mayors across Canada were asked to complete a national survey by *Leaders and Legacies*, in order to gauge municipal level support for a basic income guarantee policy. Results are slowing being released as data is gathered.

Deschenes says it's important to support people who need more income to remain above the poverty line, but she also notes that it is "everyone's responsibility to support others and sustain the region's needs."

The mayor also believes that a basic income guarantee would lead to improved individual, family and public health outcomes, and that it would stimulate the local economy in her region since more people would have more dollars to spend.

'There's a good case to be made for a basic income:' Halifax mayor

September 21, 2015

By Roderick Benns

Another big city mayor in Canada says he supports the concept of a basic income guarantee to combat inequality and create better social cohesion.

Halifax Mayor Mike Savage says "there's a good case to be made for a basic income," pointing out there are many advantages in ensuring that people have their basic needs met.

"I think we would have more social cohesion and a better balance of opportunities. We would have a narrowing of the gap between the very rich and the very poor. And we would have a more productive workforce because many would access new opportunities," says Savage, who heads the largest city in the Atlantic Region of Canada.

Savage represents the sixth provincial or territorial capital leader in Canada to support basic income policy, following the capital cities of Edmonton, Victoria, St. John, Charlottetown, and Iqaluit. As well, other big city mayors like Calgary's Naheed Nenshi and scores of small town mayors across Canada are also speaking out in favour of this issue.

The mayor – who was also a former three-term Liberal MP for Dartmouth-Cole Harbour riding – says he believes Canada should set up some pilot projects so modern data can be gathered within Canada about the effects of a guaranteed annual income.

"Pilots are absolutely essential. We need the data. It's unfortunate that we don't have the long form census which could give us good information" about where to best set up the pilots.

Savage says there must be an understanding of what programs would disappear, such as welfare or employment insurance, and what ones would be kept, even with basic income policy in place.

"There would need to be some consensus, so we're all on the same page," he says.

As a Liberal MP, Savage worked with Conservative Senator Hugh Segal and Liberal Senator Art Eggleton on issues connected to poverty and inequality. The mayor was also the critic for Human Resources Development and served on the House of Commons Standing Committee on Health. In addition, he served as the vice-chair of the standing committee on Human Resources, Social Development and the Status of Persons with Disabilities.

One of the unfortunate trends that has become more popular, says the mayor, "is speaking about the middle class."

"Nobody really defines it particularly well. I think that we all need to take more responsibility for those who are really struggling," he says.

Savage is emboldened by the "progressive group of mayors" currently helming big cities in Canada.

"We talk about these issues, like guaranteed income, housing - the broader social concerns that affect people's lives."

He says he always points out that "the feds have the money, the provinces have the jurisdiction, and the cities have the problem."

But when it comes to challenges that effect huge parts of the population, "we need to put jurisdictions aside," says Savage.

Savage says that to see the level of change that is needed around basic income, inequality, and other social policy issues, the people who are already volunteering in these sectors need to make their voices heard at the political level.

Across this country, says the mayor, people volunteer in food banks, social service groups, faith groups, and community organizations.

"Those people, especially, need to raise their voices," says Savage, because they are already active in the community.

"They need to tell the politicians that they're going to expect them to answer questions like 'are you interested in basic income?' 'Are you going to provide mental health?' 'What about housing?' Ask your MP what their plan is. I call it activating the activists," says Savage.

Back when it was more of a political issue, Savage says he was in favour of civil marriages for gays and lesbians.

"I must have heard from thousands of people on that issue. I don't think I've heard from 150 people on poverty. That will have to change if we want to see results."

Five New Brunswick mayors say it's time for basic income policy across Canada

September 23, 2015

By Roderick Benns

Five mayors from New Brunswick are speaking out in favour of basic income guarantee policy — including the mayor of Fredericton, the capital city of the province.

Brad Woodside, Mayor of Fredericton, Gerry Cormier, Mayor of Miramichi, Yvon Lapierre, Mayor of Dieppe, Cyrille Simard, Mayor of Edmundston, and Bill Bishop, Mayor of Rothesay, have all indicated various levels of support for the policy that is gaining more interest across Canada.

Mayors across Canada were given the opportunity to complete a national survey by *Leaders and Legacies*, in order to gauge municipal level support for a basic income guarantee policy.

Lapierre of Dieppe says basic income is the "best way to kick-start our economy, but only if it comes with sufficient money from the abolishment of all other social income programs, such as Employment Insurance."

A sixth mayor, Stephen Brunet of the City of Bathurst, somewhat agreed that a basic income guarantee – which would put more money in people's pockets – might stimulate the local economy of his community, which would help businesses. However, he wonders about implementation costs. Atlantic Canada support for the policy has been strong, even in the capital regions. Recently the capital city mayors of Halifax, Nova Scotia, Charlottetown, Prince Edward Island, and St. John's, Newfoundland have spoken out strongly in favour of basic income policy.

Mayors of St. Catharines, Niagara Falls declare support for basic income

September 28, 2015

By Roderick Benns

Two more Niagara-area mayors – in St. Catharines and Niagara Falls — have declared their support for basic income policy.

Mayors across Canada were given the opportunity to complete a national survey by *Leaders and Legacies*, in order to gauge municipal level support for a basic income guarantee policy. A common definition of a basic income guarantee ensures everyone an income sufficient to meet basic needs and live with dignity, regardless of work status.

Mayor Jim Diodati of Niagara Falls indicated that he supports "the idea that everyone in my city should be able to access a basic income guarantee."

He also strongly believes that a basic income guarantee "would dramatically reduce poverty" in his region, and that it would stimulate the local economy which would be helpful for the business community.

Niagara Falls is a city of 83,000 on the Canadian-U.S. border and is a major tourist destination for both Canadians and Americans. It has been undergoing major downtown revitalization projects in the last few years.

Mayor Walter Sendzik, who leads the neighbouring city of St. Catharines, also indicated "slight agreement" with a basic income guarantee, believing it would likely lead to "improved individual, family and public health outcomes" for citizens.

St. Catharines, a city of 131,000, is the largest city in the Niagara Region and sixth largest in Ontario. Like Niagara Falls, there has been is a big push for a revitalized downtown.

Earlier this month another Niagara-area mayor, Ted Luciani of Thorold, declared support for basic income policy. He noted that the "income gap between rich and poor is increasing" every moment.

"We have to start closing this gap," he says, so "let's get it done," said Luciani.

Yellowknife mayor says basic income would act like rungs to help people climb out of poverty

October 14, 2015

By Roderick Benns

The mayor of Yellowknife says it's time to set up basic income pilot projects in Canada to build on the "encouraging" Manitoba example from the 1970s.

Mayor Mark Heyck — a three-year mayor of Yellowknife, Northwest Territories, who faces re-election Oct. 19 — says basic income is "well worth looking into."

"It could provide people who have low incomes rungs to help them climb out of poverty and further their own education and their own well-being — to become stronger participants in Canadian society," he tells *Leaders and Legacies*.

Heyck is the latest Canadian mayor to be interviewed by *Leaders and Legacies,* in order to gauge municipal level support for a basic income guarantee policy. He says the example of Dauphin, Manitoba from the 1970s showed "remarkable improvements" in people's lives, after the data was analyzed. That's why he wants to see modern-day pilot projects set up, since this will also help politicians to be able to sell the vision afterwards, assuming the data is encouraging.

The mayor was born and raised in the territory's capital city area, situated on the northern shores of Great Slave Lake. While the climate is subarctic here, the debate over poverty is heating up as talk of living wages has been in the local news lately, and now basic income.

According to a Northern News Services report in 2013, the Territory boasts Canada's highest Gross Domestic Product at $3.52 million, as well as the highest individual incomes in Canada. However, the income gap between the territory's richest and poorest residents is vast. The territory's richest residents have an annual income of more than $200,000 a year, while its poorest live on less than $18,000 per year. Sixteen per cent of all families in the Territory earn less than $30,000 a year, according to the report on poverty cited by Northern News.

Heyck says Yellowknife, with 20,000 people, is the hub for programs and services for the whole territory.

"The economy is very strong here. Our unemployment rate typically hovers at around four percent," says Heyck. "Finding a job in Yellowknife is relatively simple – although that can sometimes mean holding down two or three jobs in the services sector."

Smaller Communities

The mayor says that many people "come here from small communities to access services or to find economic opportunity."

"Sometimes that works out and sometimes it doesn't," he says. Often, he says, the people who are homeless in Yellowknife have come from other smaller communities looking for opportunity in the capital.

The challenge for northerners, says the mayor, "is dealing with the cost of living up here." Like in all areas of Canada, "social assistance doesn't make the cut" in terms of adequately providing for people. As well, there are housing concerns in Yellowknife where the average price for a two bedroom apartment is $1600.

According to a 2014 CBC News story, 'Northern Property' owns almost three-quarters of rental properties in Yellowknife. Last year the company complained that two-thirds of its tenants who were on income assistance were behind in rent payments.

There is a long list for social housing, the mayor admits, and that's why the City has "put a great deal of emphasis on ensuring higher density" in housing, with more affordable housing units, ranging from $200-220,000 to ensure there is an opportunity for first time home buyers.

Being able to count on a basic income, he says, would allow people "to focus on their education, or issues that come up in their lives."

"They can persevere through these obstacles because they know they will be able to make it financially," he says, if such a policy were in place.

Mayor of Whitehorse says basic income pilot projects the best way forward

October 31, 2015

By Roderick Benns

The mayor of Whitehorse, Yukon, the recently re-elected Dan Curtis, says the challenges of northern living make investigating a basic income guarantee a viable idea.

Curtis says he "would love to see everyone in the middle class, but it's challenging when there is so much work in the (lower paying) service industry," even with people often working two or more jobs to make ends meet.

Curtis is the latest Canadian mayor to be interviewed by *Leaders and Legacies,* in order to gauge municipal level support for a basic income guarantee policy.

"It's a real concern to see people like this remain above the poverty line. So I would be very interested in investigating this (basic income) policy to see what would be viable."

The mayor says it makes sense to him to set up pilot projects first so things can be tested. "That's the way to go. Trying a pilot project out would let us see any pitfalls and measure the successes."

Housing

Like many northern communities, Curtis says Whitehorse is "challenged with affordable housing." He points out there are 114 families in his city currently looking for sustainable, affordable places to live.

On the other hand – and echoing comments made by Yellowknife Mayor Mark Heyck – Curtis says there is "tremendous opportunity" in Whitehorse, particularly for those able to work for one of the four levels of government – federal, territorial, municipal, or First Nations.

"Many people are doing quite well and then others are struggling," says Curtis. It is that inequality gap that has him concerned.

Curtis says as an example, Whitehorse's Filipino community is about 3,000 strong. "Many of these folks rely on family and friends to help one another out, and most are working two or three jobs," but finding affordable housing is still an issue for them.

"Many are also attending Yukon College at the same time," to try and better themselves.

"They are a fantastic addition to our community," but the housing situation for the Filipino community — and for other people on the waiting list – is not sustainable, he says.

When asked about the viability of creating a limited basic income for the Yukon Territory, such as the Alaskan Dividend in the nearby U.S. state, Curtis points out that the territory doesn't have a lot of resources, excluding its modest gold production and some other minerals. All of Alaska's dividend comes straight from oil profits.

Curtis says setting up pilot projects to determine the viability of a basic income program will "get any uncertainty out of the way."

All three territorial capital mayors have now indicated their support for investigating basic income policy as way to address growing inequality gaps in Canada's north.

Saskatchewan Green Party leader believes basic income on table after 2016 election

November 4, 2015

Roderick Benns recently interviewed Victor Lau, the leader of the Green Party of Saskatchewan, about basic income.

Benns: *Do you run candidates in all ridings?*

Lau: Yes — the Green Party of Saskatchewan ran our first full slate of 58 candidates in the previous general election in 2011. For 2016, our party finished nominating a full slate of 61 candidates (the provincial government added three more seats) by the summer of 2014. We are currently the only party in Saskatchewan to have finished nominating their entire slate of candidates. Even the Saskatchewan Party government has two more seats to go and the NDP has just over half of theirs done.

Benns: *Are there any signs of electoral success on the horizon for any of your candidates?*

Lau: The Green Party of Saskatchewan believes strongly that by being ready with a full slate of 61 candidates and an excellent platform for 2016 that our central messaging should carry us to victory in three to four seats or potentially even propel us into forming government (only 31 seats are needed to do so.)

Benns: *Tell me a bit about yourself. Do you have any lived experience with poverty?*

Lau: Well my parents both immigrated to Canada from China/Hong Kong. I am their first born child and a first generation Canadian. I have grown up in Regina, Saskatchewan and see myself as a prairie boy. My family started out with very, very modest means, so we did live very plainly but I never felt poor. My parents were both excellent cooks and fabulous providers so our family, through hard work, managed to overcome our poorer circumstances. It's a very successful story similar to many new immigrant families who arrive in Canada.

Benns: *How did you come to advocate for this kind of change and much more through the Green's?*

Lau: The first time I heard of the guaranteed income was via a documentary video called 'Sex, Drugs and Democracy.' It was from the 1990s and showed how the Netherlands was a virtual utopia. As an impressionable youth in my twenties, looking for a way to create a more 'just society,' this video seemed to point the way forward — especially on poverty elimination. It seemed too good to be true and when I got a chance to talk to an actual citizen of the Netherlands, he confirmed that the guaranteed income was not free of means testing/work requirements (such as in the form of mandatory volunteerism) so the video was kind of stretching the reality a bit.

As for why the Green Party, I started my political advocacy as an NDPer, having been influenced by an incredibly kind man named Ed Whelan, a former cabinet minister in both the Douglas and Blakeney governments, and his book *Touched by Tommy*. I lasted four years in the NDP, even becoming youth leader at their 50th anniversary celebration in 1994. But I gave up on the party when all my friends had abandoned the NDP during the disappointing Roy Romanow era. In 1997-98, a group of disaffected NDP'ers and Greens came together and petitioned to form a new party. At first it was called the New Green Alliance, but later renamed in 2006 to the Green Party of Saskatchewan.

Benns: *Why is the concept of a basic income guarantee so important at this point in our societal development?*

Lau: Three trends come to mind as to why a guaranteed basic income is so very important. First, the growing amount of seniors in Canada and the many, many retirees from the baby boomer generation. Second, the incredibly fast shift towards more and more automation and part-time employment. Third, most — if not all — governments are carrying huge debt loads and their health care budgets are stretched to the maximum.

Taking just all three of the above points (not to mention our economy and our environment) most people can sense a need for an entire overhaul of our social safety net in Canada. A guaranteed basic income would help alleviate the stress in all three categories plus move our common society forward towards compassion for all by eliminating the ugly stigma of being on welfare. If we all share in society's prosperity via a universal guaranteed livable income, then like Medicare, it will become treasured as a foundation for Canada's continued leadership in social reform and innovation.

Benns: *A recent poverty task force in Saskatchewan has recommended a basic income policy of some kind. Do you feel that this recommendation will be ignored or is there some hope for it to be adopted?*

Lau: I strongly believe that whomever forms government after April 4, 2016 will strive towards implementing a guaranteed income.

The Saskatchewan Party did the right thing by separating disabled people from abled people in the welfare system, and putting them on SAID (Saskatchewan Assured Income for the Disabled). It's somewhat similar to Alberta's Assured Income for the Severely Handicapped (AISH) program.

Now the opposition NDP has recently come on board to support a guaranteed basic income pilot project. This is a huge movement from their 2011 position of supporting only the status quo welfare system.

Then you have the Saskatchewan Green Party which has been in favour of implementing a guaranteed livable income since the party's inception in 1999. This means that all three major parties in Saskatchewan generally support transforming welfare into a different state. Only the Green Party would move directly to full implementation and not just do a test pilot. But the political desire is there; it remains to be seen if the political will can be mustered and that's where the electorate comes in. We plan to make guaranteed livable income and poverty elimination a major issue in the 2016 general election.

Benns: *How can citizens help bring about the kind of change needed like basic income?*

Lau: The main thing citizens can do is spread the word, have discussions with friends and neighbours, talk about how and why a guaranteed livable income would make life easier for everyone and cost the provincial and national government less.

Benns: *The social determinants of health are vital in understanding how some people are set up to succeed in life and others to fail – because of social structures we have created. What are a couple of Green policies that would really help more people succeed – for society to be more just?*

Lau: One of the big policies is implementing a guaranteed livable income. This would free citizens to be active participants in their own destiny.

By showing people we have more in common, we build a more united and prosperous province for all who come here and raise families here. It really is a once in a lifetime opportunity to elect a government that is truly committed to real change that will last for generations to come.

Basic income should be a core value, like health care: Michael Clague

November 6, 2015

By Roderick Benns

Michael Clague grew up as a middle class boy in Vancouver, B.C. in the 1940s. He was fortunate, he says, because he never had to experience poverty firsthand. Given that his father was a school principal in an east Vancouver school, though, he did encounter a number of people who came from families with low incomes.

But it wasn't until many years later, when he was appointed to the Special Senate Committee on Poverty, that Clague would realize the weight of poverty that existed for many. Chaired by Senator David Croll in 1968, the final report says it well:

"The Committee travelled the length and breadth of Canada on a fact-finding assignment without parallel in our history. Its members saw the tragedy of poverty first hand; not in abstract terms but in the crucible of human experience."

In a bold, declarative style that still stands as a vital report nearly 50 years later after it was published, the report chronicled poverty in Canada in a way that hadn't been done before. It also declared that Canada was ready for a basic income guarantee:

"It is the Committee's recommendation that the Parliament of Canada...provide a guaranteed minimum income for all Canadians with insufficient income. This includes the...unemployed, those whose incomes are too low because they work in seasonal occupations, and those who are victims of jobs where the pay is insufficient to provide for their basic needs."

Clague, now retired, would spend his life working in community development after this landmark report. At one time he was president of the Canadian Council on Social Development in Ottawa, which saw its funding cut during the last ten years of Conservative governments. When he thinks back to some of the writing he contributed to the report on social planning and in other segments, he says a basic income guarantee was its "signal recommendation."

"The report makes the case for getting rid of some aspects of the welfare income support state and replacing it with a guaranteed annual income," he tells *Leaders and Legacies*.

Clague believed then in a basic income guarantee and he still believes it. He says that "in a good society, we all contribute something, however modest, and therefore we should all benefit from our contribution."

He says the reasons for basic income "are as compelling to me today as they were then."

"It's an opportunity to simplify a complex system. It would provide an incentive for employment transition to those who are capable of employment, as opposed to the disincentive of welfare. Those are powerful reasons."

Given the nature of precarious work, says Clague, with contracts, part time jobs, and work with no benefits, with basic income guarantee policy people could move from one working opportunity to another without undue hardship.

Like Health Care

Clague says that to 'sell' basic income to society, "we have to figure out how to make it meaningful to the general public."

"I do think it's tied to the idea of universality. If it's understood that all Canadians, like we have with health care, are assured of core financial security if they get in trouble, it makes it more saleable."

"Even if my earning is minimum," says Clague, "I'm still paying taxes into the general welfare of the country. It's a notion that in a good society we all contribute and will all benefit. That's why universality is so important. Income is re-distributed universally according to your needs."

Clague says we need two kinds of overarching policy. One addresses issues of survival – the basic income we all need – and the other addresses issues of choice.

"When my income is sufficient then I am able to make choices – choices of the jobs I choose, the education I pursue, and how I contribute to society."

"Income is for survival. Income re-distribution is to give people the chance to make choices."

Kingston woman says Canada spends more money managing poverty than it would cost to eliminate it

November 9, 2015

Roderick Benns recently interviewed Tara Kainer, a long-time anti-poverty advocate, about basic income guarantee policy.

Tara Kainer grew up talking about social justice issues around the dinner table. In the 1950s, when she was a small child, her family lived in Tennessee where segregation was still in place and poverty, especially in the rural areas, was extreme.

Because her mother worked in the emergency department of a local hospital she often talked about the people who were turned away from medical services because they couldn't pay. After leaving Tennessee they lived in Saskatchewan where the CCF government brought in Medicare before it was adopted by the federal government in 1966. Her parents were fervent supporters.

As an adult and single mother of three sons, she moved from Saskatchewan to Ontario to enrol in a PhD program but wasn't able to finish. Because she didn't yet have a network of contacts in Kingston, she couldn't find decent work. Instead, she pieced together a series of part-time, freelance, and contract jobs which didn't pay the rent and put food on the table. As a result she ended up on social assistance.

During those years she volunteered for an anti-poverty group and learned how to advocate for herself and others. While she continued to work, even a full-time job at a book store didn't pay enough to sustain her and her family. It took eight years before she was able to find a decent job, first as a housing support worker at a local housing provider, then as support staff in the social justice office of the Sisters of Providence of St. Vincent de Paul. Only then was she able to exit the welfare system.

Benns: *What about basic income policy makes it a smart move for the economy?*

Kainer: Of all the supports on offer to people living in poverty, a guaranteed annual income made the most sense to me. It still does. Canada currently spends more money managing poverty than it would eradicating it through a basic income guarantee. The patchwork of support systems currently in place – from tax revenue-generated programs like social assistance to charitable enterprises like food banks and meal programs – costs society billions of dollars a year.

In health care dollars alone poverty costs Canada over $7 billion dollars annually. But the overall economic and social costs of poverty to both the poor and non-poor alike, which include lost productivity, opportunity and potential; homelessness, addictions, domestic violence, policing, prisons and other social control measures, was estimated by the Ontario Association of Food Banks in 2008 to be between $72 and $86 billion a year.

In 2013 the Fraser Institute calculated the total cost of Canada's current income support system (payout plus administrative costs) at $185-billion. A guaranteed annual income would be a bargain by comparison: the cost of providing every adult with an annual income of $20,000 and children with an income guarantee of $6,000, the Basic Income Guarantee group in Kingston gauges, would come to about $40-billion.

My greatest worry and regret about having lived in poverty is the effect it had on my children. While their peers had music lessons, joined sports teams, and travelled the world, my sons missed out on one opportunity after another, ate less nutritious food than they should have, made do with second-hand clothes, lived in tiny, overcrowded apartments. Poverty is soul-destroying. It's impossible to put a price tag on that.

Benns: *What about a basic income guarantee makes it a social justice issue?*

Kainer: If we are ever to create an equitable society — meaning a healthy, inclusive, productive society –we have to address the Social Determinants of Health (SDoH). The Canadian Medical Association says the social conditions in which we live determine our health and well-being more than any other factor, whether that is our biology, environment, or health care. Level of income is at the top of the list of the SDoH followed by early childhood development, disability, education, social inclusion, social safety net, gender, Aboriginal status, race, safe nutritious food, housing/homelessness, and community belonging.

A basic income policy would establish an income floor just above the poverty line which would ensure that all Canadians meet their basic needs. It would stabilize lives and end the chronic insecurity low-income Canadians are experiencing now. Not having to constantly worry about money and the consequences of poverty an inadequate income brings would improve health and overall quality of life, enable people to live in peace and with dignity, feel a part of society, and leave people free to follow higher educations, better jobs, and creative pursuits.

A professor and co-president of the Basic Income Earth Network, Guy Standing, says rapid technological changes are leading to huge job losses and the creation of a burgeoning social class. Standing calls them "the precariat" and this is another reason for implementing a basic income guarantee. Increasingly, in a world where there are self-driving cars and airplanes, and robots that can fill prescriptions, analyze documents, greet shoppers, operate on patients in hospitals and care for the elderly in nursing homes, it will make sense to separate income from labour.

Benns: *The most common concern about implementing a basic income guarantee is that too many of us would choose not to work. Why do you believe this won't be the case?*

Kainer: In my experience, the vast majority of people are not content to merely survive on subsistence incomes. They will do their utmost to improve the quality of their lives. When I worked 40 hours a week, all-year round, for eight years on assistance, my earnings were clawed back by the Ontario government. In exchange I was topped up with about $150 a month over and above my wages and was able to keep dental benefits for my kids and a drug card for my family. Not a lot of financial compensation for the work I was doing.

But it was the satisfaction I got from getting out into the public every day, conversing with my peers, and feeling that I was contributing to society that made working well worth it. I knew others who volunteered when they couldn't work, or spent their spare time when they weren't hustling to merely survive acquiring knowledge and learning new skills. Very, very few fit the stereotype of welfare recipients sitting at home waiting for their next cheque to arrive.

A basic income, Standing says in the same article cited above, "would not reduce labour supply." His basic income guarantee pilot projects in India, as well as Mincome in Canada, and others in the US and several European countries, have demonstrated that "people with basic security work harder and more productively, not less." They move from a position of despair that chronic poverty brings to one of hope. People who are secure in knowing they have enough income to cover their basic needs feel more in control of their lives and experience better health. Less uncertainty, chaos, and confusion frees them to think about matters other than basic survival and inspires them to more and better things. That was certainly the case for me.

Economics professor says evidence shows basic income grants used responsibly

November 11, 2015

Roderick Benns recently interviewed Robin Boadway, a retired economics professor. Boadway studied economics at Oxford University on a Rhodes Scholarship. He has his doctorate in economics from Queen's University in Kingston.

Benns: *How did you come to be involved in this issue?*

Boadway: I spent my academic career as a public finance economist studying optimal policies for achieving a just and fair society, particularly with regard to those most in need. Naturally, guaranteed annual income is one important element of redistributive policies. I was especially influenced by economists like Anthony Atkinson and Amartya Sen for whom basic income was both fair and conducive to equality of opportunity.

The views of philosopher John Rawls were also influential, particularly the idea that societal outcomes owe much to luck at birth, and those of us who are luckier than others owe it to the less fortunate to share in our luck. Having spent most of my life teaching and studying the importance of a basic income guarantee, the BIG group in Kingston offered an irresistible opportunity to have some practical effect.

Benns: *You're a retired economics professor -what about basic income policy makes it a smart move for the economy?*

Boadway: Poverty is wasteful, not only in terms of loss of economic value but more importantly because of loss of personal and family fulfillment. A policy of basic income for all would induce a change in social values and norms, including by recipients. It would improve self-esteem and reduce stigmatization; it would encourage and enable the disadvantaged to lead more productive lives; it would reduce anti-social behaviour; and it would help eliminate the poverty trap that is passed on from generation to generation.

Benns: *What about a basic income guarantee makes it a social justice issue?*

Boadway: To me, freedom from poverty and satisfactions of basic needs are fundamental human rights. They are also a prerequisite to participating meaningfully in society. As well, as I have mentioned, those of us who are more affluent than average owe our success in good part to luck rather than merit. This includes where and when we were born, our native abilities, our family backgrounds, the opportunities made available to us, and so on. We owe it to the less fortunate to share our good fortune.

Benns: *The most common concern about implementing a basic income is that too many of us would choose not to work.*

Boadway: Evidence from guaranteed basic income experiments indicates that those who receive grants do not squander it. Some use it to provide better outcomes for their children. Others use it to support improving their own skills. Very few simply become idle and live off the grant. This is not surprising. Basic income is not designed to give recipients a luxurious life. There will always be a desire to earn income over and above the basic income guarantee level in order to achieve personal and family fulfillment.

Existing welfare programs are not good indicators of behaviour under a basic income. They are rife with stigmatization and impose strong penalties to work and save. It is possible to design the system so that recipients retain an incentive to undertake productive activity, including work, entrepreneurship and education.

Hugh Segal inspires basic income advocates

November 16, 2015

By Roderick Benns

Retired Conservative Senator Hugh Segal energized about 50 Ontario advocates of a basic income guarantee on Saturday who were looking for inspiration and advice from one of the great leaders of the movement.

Segal didn't disappoint, bringing his trademark humour and optimism in support of a cause he has championed for 40 years. He says a "confluence of events" has produced an incredible window of opportunity for basic income policy and that it was time to "seize this moment."

"At no point in the last 40 years have I been as optimistic as I am now," says Segal.

He says the election of this particular federal Liberal government is the latest sign of optimism, given that newly-elected Prime Minister Justin Trudeau has instructed his Minister of Families, Children and Social Development, Jean-Yves Duclos, to commit to the relief of poverty on a national scale as a top priority of his mandate.

Other indicators of a building interest in a basic income guarantee include:

- The election of an NDP government in Alberta, which was once a Conservative bastion
- The support of an increasing number of mayors across Canada, including big city mayors like Don Iveson of Edmonton, Naheed Nenshi of Calgary, and Mike Savage of Halifax, who see the effects of poverty firsthand in their communities

- The election of an Ontario Liberal government that is keen on bold poverty reduction measures
- The support of an increasing number of health-related organizations, such as the Ontario Public Health Association and the Canadian Medical Association.
- The poverty reduction report solicited by the Saskatchewan government and its recommendation to support a basic income policy
- The election of a Liberal government in Prince Edward Island earlier this year that indicated its support for basic income during the campaign

Despite governments spending billions of dollars on the downstream effects of poverty — like poor education outcomes, youth involved with crime, domestic violence, and the outcome of poor diets — poverty has persisted for Canadians under the age of 65.

Segal says a breakthrough for the basic income movement would be the creation of multiple pilot projects across the country. He says he likes the fact that it was former Prime Minister Pierre Trudeau who initiated the Dauphin, Manitoba experiment on basic income in the 1970s, even though he eventually failed to analyze the results. Segal sees it as fitting that Pierre Trudeau's son has the opportunity to restart pilots on an even larger, more useful scale to gather the data over five years which will help build political will for the policy.

Segal, who is now the Master of Massey College, says the fact that health economics researcher, Dr. Evelyn Forget, is now a visiting scholar there to study basic income is also a great opportunity for the movement. Forget is taking the lead on an investigation into the results from the mid-1970's Mincome Guaranteed Annual Income experiment in Dauphin.

The former Tory senator says it is imperative to get the business community involved and on side with the idea of basic income, noting the Conference Board of Canada has been advocating for a basic income.

Segal says if all goes according to plan for those who support this policy, he envisions the federal Liberals doing a Speech from the Throne half way through their first term in office which would kick-start pilot programs. By then, the Liberals would have seen more international evidence coming in that supports basic income, as well as having been briefed on efforts in cities and provinces across Canada to try out this new approach to social policy.

"If we think about Tommy Douglas" in Saskatchewan, says Segal, referring to the father of Medicare, in Canada, "he faced a long list of arguments as to why health care couldn't happen."

That's what is happening with basic income in some circles, says Segal.

For instance, the Fraser Institute, known for its support of right wing policies, came out with a thoughtful, well-researched report on basic income last year which states the idea of basic income was appealing. However, they concluded the political will was not there, given the complexities of multiple levels of governments needing to cooperate.

"But things have changed," says Segal, given the shifts in governments across Canada and an emerging groundswell of support from many organizations. "I think we now truly have reason to be optimistic."

Enough fear, poverty, bureaucracy: U.S. advocate, Santens, says basic income is the answer

November 19, 2015

Roderick Benns recently interviewed Scott Santens, one of the leading American voices for basic income. The New Orleans-based writer is an advocate of basic income for all people and he serves as moderator of the BasicIncome community on Reddit.

Benns: *The very notion of a basic income guarantee frightens a lot of people, particularly in western societies like Canada and the U.S. Thinking of employers, how can they be convinced that basic income policy is a good idea? Won't they be worried about finding people willing to work?*

Santens: It's kind of interesting isn't it, that the asking of such a question directly implies that employers don't actually pay workers sufficiently for them to work voluntarily. We all know that's the case, but we ignore it. The rate employers currently pay for the jobs people don't want to do is artificially low. It's low because people have to choose between no money at all, and at least some money. That's coercion. It's an imbalance of bargaining power. It's also a market distortion.

Employers have no incentive to pay sufficient wages, so people accept insufficient wages and consider themselves lucky they don't have to live hungry in a box in an alley somewhere. Because people are willing to accept such low wages to the point they will be the working poor, the government steps in with further market distorting regulations like the minimum wage. But then this wage fixing also affects jobs that people would actually be happy to accept less than the minimum, because that job provides meaning. Perhaps it's an exciting start-up. Perhaps it's something requiring few hours.

But unfortunately the business can't afford the mandated wage, thanks to the other employers that refused to pay sufficient wages.

With that said, employers can be convinced basic income is a good idea for a few powerful reasons:

One: A nationally-mandated minimum wage would become optional. Employers that would have to raise their wages because those jobs have so little demand may not be so happy about this, but employers with jobs that have great demand may be, because they could stop giving raises thanks to a basic income indexed to rise with at least the annual rate of inflation, but even better, productivity. Basically, the labour market would be transformed into an actual market, where crap jobs are recognized with good pay, and great jobs are recognized as being intrinsically, not extrinsically motivated.

Two: Flexibility in hiring and firing should be very interesting to employers. Denmark is considered the best country in the world for business because of its 'Flexicurity' system where there is essentially both flexibility and security. The easier the government makes it for people to move from job to job, the easier it can be to fire unwanted labour in favour of wanted labour. Flexicurity has nothing on Unconditional Basic Income. With basic income, there are no forms to fill out. There's no application process. There's no gaps in coverage. There's no getting the wrong amount. Everyone always has basic income. All of this means businesses can be allowed far more flexibility in their staffing decisions, and would thus be far more competitive against inflexible competitors.

Three: The biggest reason of all for businesses to support basic income is about as simple as it gets — customers. More people with more money means more customers with more spending power. Basic income should sound like 'cha-ching' to any owner of a business whose business isn't built on the economic suffering of others, e.g. payday loan lenders and private prisons.

Benns: *Automation is taking away many jobs, but there are vast swaths of jobs that still need filling, such as those in the service sectors. How will they attract people if BI is in place?*

Santens: Again, it is up to the employer to offer wages to humans sufficient for humans to non-coercively accept those wages thanks to the actual ability to say no to them. If because of this, the hourly wage of human labour for a job rises from $7 to $20, and the effective cost for a machine to do that job instead is $10, then it now makes far more economic sense to hand that labour over to the process of automation. And this is really the result we all should want because it means on one hand that more people are now free to do meaningful work, and on the other hand it means employees who will work 24 hours a day 7 days a week, who will never strike and who no longer require any benefits of any kind. Machines are the perfect employees. Let's welcome them so we can move on to bigger and better things, like being human.

Benns: *What are some first practical steps we can take as a society to implement basic income?*

Santens: The biggest barrier to basic income happening tomorrow is that however more frequently it is being mentioned all over the world, it has not yet reached the point of being known by anything close to even half the population. Everyone knows what minimum wage is. Everyone knows what tax cuts are. Not even close to everyone knows what universal basic income is. So the first practical step is to talk about it. Help get the idea out there. Share article after article. Use sites like basicincome.org and reddit.com/r/basicincome as resources. Start conversations.

Ask people, 'What would you do if enough money showed up in your bank account every month for you to never worry about meeting your basic needs?' Get people thinking how this would impact their lives. If you're an organization, publicly express your support for the idea, just as in Canada the Canadian Medical Association and Food

Banks Canada have. Another practical step is to connect with others who also feel the idea is important. Connect online and also in person. Join a local group. Start one if there isn't one. Organize a Basic Income Create-A-Thon.

Additionally, call your local political representatives on the phone, and tell them you support it. If they have no idea what it is, explain it to them. The more they hear about it, the more they will feel it's in their best interests to start talking about it themselves.

Benns: *Why is the concept of a basic income guarantee so important at this point in our societal development?*

Santens: We're living in a paradox of absurdity, where we've created truly incredible levels of technology, growing at exponential rates, and yet we're not using it to propel our civilization forward. Technology has from the moment the first tool was ever created, been intended to reduce human labour. And yet here we are working 47 hours a week instead of 40, and working nine hours a day at the office despite not actually working for four of them. We're encouraging people to work in jobs they hate instead of doing work they love. We've increased the risks of failure, putting a counterproductive brake on innovation. We're increasing inequality, hampering our economies.

We're reducing bargaining power by decreasing the ability to say no. And we're replacing human workers with technologies that don't buy anything. None of this makes any sense if our goal is for technology to work for us instead of against us. So let's do that instead. Let's leverage technology to free us. Enough fear. Enough poverty. Enough bureaucracy. Enough crap jobs. Enough wasted human potential. Enough is enough. It's time to remove the brakes and let this civilization fly.

Why the Liberals should institute a basic income guarantee

December 5, 2015

By Roderick Benns

When Prime Minister Justin Trudeau gave his ministers their marching orders shortly after taking office, he instructed Families, Children and Social Development Minister Jean-Yves Duclos to make relieving poverty on a national scale a top priority. But did he mean for that to eventually take the form of a basic income guarantee?

A basic income guarantee is known by many names, including a guaranteed annual income, a minimum income and a negative income tax, among others. But the essence is that it ensures everyone an income that is sufficient to meet their basic needs, regardless of work status. It provides a direct cash transfer to the people who most need economic security. The policy has fans across the political spectrum, with some intrigued at the premise of eradicating poverty and others enamoured with the idea of eliminating massive bureaucracies, such as the welfare system.

Minister Duclos, an economist by training, signalled strong support for a basic income guarantee in a 2008 Institute for Research on Public Policy brief. The essence of his proposal was to replace all existing tax transfers, allowances and social assistance "with a basic income transfer, which would be available to all working-age Canadians but whose net value would decline with rising levels of income." This new basic income would be federally financed and administered through the personal income tax system.

This is a policy that was tested in Canada in the 1970s, in the small town of Dauphin, Man. Its success was later documented by researcher Evelyn Forget. While issues like "living wages" are currently getting most of the media play, a basic income guarantee is quickly catching up in the public consciousness. For instance, the current Liberal government in Prince Edward Island, which was elected earlier this year and led by Premier Wade MacLauchlan, went so far as to call for a model program and promised to "build in a commitment to evidence-based research and action-based research."

From the province that brought us health care, Saskatchewan Premier Brad Wall's government is currently considering its own poverty task force's recommendation to set up a basic income to help stamp out poverty. The Canadian Medical Association and Ontario health units also like the idea of a basic income.

Basic income is on the radar of Canada's mayors, too, who often see the effects of poverty firsthand in their communities and are asking for new tools in order to create real change. In fact, no less than nine provincial and territorial capitals have spoken out in favour of the policy.

Internationally, countries such as Finland and the Netherlands are currently setting up pilot projects to measure the impact a basic income would have.

For his part, Duclos is currently trumpeting the federal Liberals' new enhanced, progressive Child Tax Benefit, which is certainly a form of basic income — as is Canada's Old Age Security system, at the other end of the age spectrum. What's missing is secure coverage for everyone in between.

In a radio interview with Evan Solomon earlier this month, Duclos didn't commit to a basic income policy when asked directly about it, but neither did he rule it out. Instead, he said that "if ever it were implemented, we'd need some strong cooperation with the provinces."

Last year at a federal Liberal policy conference, two resolutions were passed by the delegates. One resolution called for testing this basic income approach, the other for full design and implementation.

As Duclos works towards lifting hundreds of thousands of Canadians out of poverty, he would do well to revive his own thinking on this issue and get the ear of his prime minister, as this is a policy that would not only help to eliminate poverty, it is also a solution for a staid economy, because it would increase the spending power of low income Canadians.

This article was originally published in The National Post.

A basic income should be considered a human right, advocates say

December 10, 2015

By Roderick Benns

On International Human Rights Day, a Perth, Ontario man says he believes a basic income guarantee for all should be one of those human rights.

Rob Rainer, a well-known basic income advocate, says he believes that basic income is a means "to help ensure that such internationally recognized social and economic rights as the right to food, housing and a standard of living adequate for the health of oneself and one's family, are honoured and protected."

A basic income guarantee is known by many names, including a guaranteed annual income, a minimum income and a negative income tax, among others. But the essence is that it ensures everyone an income that is sufficient to meet their basic needs, regardless of work status. It provides a direct cash transfer to the people who most need economic security.

"The principal reason I am fighting for a basic income guarantee," says Rainer, "is that I believe, deeply, that basic income should be a human right. That's part of why the international Human Rights Day is so important to me."

Joe Foster, a long-time basic income advocate from the Kingston area, says we shouldn't "miss the opportunity to respond to the greatest violation of Human Rights — the lack of sufficient funds to meet basic needs."

Foster believes a new and "enlightened" federal government will allow for the possibility of this message to get through. He points out Article 25 within the Universal Declaration on Human Rights, which was proclaimed by the United Nations General Assembly on this day in Paris in 1948:

"Everyone has the right to a standard of living adequate for the health and well-being of himself and of his family, including food, clothing, housing, and medical care and necessary social services, and the right to security in the event of unemployment, sickness, disability, widowhood, old age or other lack of livelihood in circumstances beyond his control."

Foster says, "In light of changes that have been brought about by globalization and technology, a basic income is the logical and efficient way to move towards eliminating poverty. Canada has the capability to do this."

Rainer agrees. He notes that the Declaration of Human Rights and related international human rights law represent, in the words of former Supreme Court of Canada Justice Louise Arbour, "an international consensus on the minimum conditions for a life of dignity."

It's Rainer's intent to help "make 2016 a breakthrough year for gaining a basic income guarantee for everyone in Canada."

Kingston the first Canadian municipality to call for basic income guarantee

December 16, 2015

By Roderick Benns

The City of Kingston has become the first municipality in Canada to call for the development of a basic income guarantee for all Canadians.

Council recently and unanimously passed a motion calling for a national discussion on the issue, hoping this will lead the provinces and federal government to work together to "consider, investigate, and develop a Basic Income Guarantee for all Canadians."

A basic income guarantee is known by many names, including a guaranteed annual income, a minimum income and a negative income tax, among others. But the essence is that it ensures everyone an income that is sufficient to meet their basic needs, regardless of work status. It provides a direct cash transfer to the people who most need economic security.

Kingston Mayor Bryan Paterson says he believes a basic income "appeals to both the left and right on the political spectrum."

"It's a question of reaching out to those in need, but also in doing this in the most efficient way possible," Paterson tells *Leaders and Legacies*, and basic income policy seems to meet both desired outcomes.

The mayor, an economist by training, says there is a sense that current system is inefficient and that there are better ways to spend tax dollars and make them go further. He acknowledges there are a lot of questions about how it might look, and how to transition from the current patchwork system of benefits.

Paterson points out that his municipality sees "the challenges with the current system," including "the disincentives for work."

As an example, he says that under the current welfare model people "are penalized for having assets."

"A basic income guarantee wouldn't do that," he says, so someone doesn't have to be completely destitute to receive some help.

The 2011 National Household Survey showed that 14.9 percent of the Canadian population lives in low income circumstances, a percentage exceeded in Kingston where the percentage is closer to 15.4 percent.

The mayor says Kingston resident and former Conservative Senator, Hugh Segal, has been out front on this issue for decades, and that a "number of community members have reached out personally to me to encourage this (motion)."

In the motion that passed, Council pointed out a number of converging factors and reasons to support basic income, including income insecurity, precarious employment, inequality, and adverse public health outcomes for people living in poverty. All of which, in turn, can lead to low levels of education, chronic stress, and criminal activity, which is more costly than poverty in the long run.

Long List of Mayors

Paterson joins a long list of other mayors across Canada who are speaking out in favour of the policy change, including big city mayors like Calgary's Naheed Nenshi, Edmonton Mayor Don Iveson, and Halifax Mayor Mike Savage.

He says the Kingston resolution will be forwarded to all municipalities in Ontario with the request that they consider indicating their own support for the initiative. It will also be forwarded to the Association of Municipalities of Ontario and the Federation of Canadian Municipalities. The hope is that these groups will engage with the provincial and federal governments to further its case.

Other indicators of a building interest in a basic income guarantee include:

- The election of an NDP government in Alberta, which was once a Conservative bastion
- Families, Children and Social Development Minister Jean-Yves Duclos, an economist by training, signalled strong support for a basic income guarantee in a 2008 Institute for Research on Public Policy brief, as first published in the Post.
- The election of an Ontario Liberal government that is keen on bold poverty reduction measures
- The support of an increasing number of health-related organizations, such as the Ontario Public Health Association and the Canadian Medical Association.
- The poverty reduction report solicited by the Saskatchewan government and its recommendation to support a basic income policy
- The election of a Liberal government in Prince Edward Island earlier this year that indicated its support for basic income during the campaign

Building a society trumps the economy, says retired planner

December 23, 2015

Roderick Benns recently interviewed Alan Gummo, a retired city and regional planner. Gummo was also a public policy researcher and worked in municipal administration. He is active in the basic income movement and now divides his time between Kingston, Ontario and Sao Paulo, Brazil.

Benns: *How did you come to be involved with advocating for a basic income guarantee?*

Gummo: I first learned of the BIG concept (Basic Income Guarantee) when I was in grad school in the 1970s. The Dauphin pilot project was on our curriculum. It sounded like a logical 'next step' in the evolution of progressive public policy. I was disappointed when the pilot was abandoned. Indeed I was disappointed with a large number of public policy decisions that were made over the following decades and seemed to take us away from a progressive direction.

I retired from my career at the end of 2012 and discovered that BIG was back on the agenda. I was introduced to a local volunteer advocacy group by an old friend. I joined the group. I should also mention that I've had the opportunity to spend extended periods of time in Brazil over the past decade or so. This has given me the opportunity to look into the Bolsa Familia, a national program equivalent to BIG that has helped raise millions out of poverty. So I know that BIG can work 'as advertised.'

Benns: *What about basic income policy makes it a smart move for the economy?*

Gummo: The benefits of BIG are social and economic. There is a popular misconception that society and economy are somehow separate. In fact they are seamlessly linked. We need an approach to public policy that is holistic, that embraces society and economy — as well as culture and environment — and seeks to create benefits and manage costs across all four areas of concentration.

There is a second popular misconception — that the economy is somehow paramount to society, and that the rules of the marketplace should drive the social agenda. In fact the economy is a subset of society, not the other way around. When all social and economic considerations are factored in, as has been done elsewhere by a credible crew of experts in such fields as economics, public health, education, and public policy, a properly designed BIG program is shown to be smart for both society and the economy. Indeed it is persisting with the status-quo that is 'not smart.'

Benns: *The most common concern about implementing a basic income guarantee is that too many of us would choose not to work. Why do you believe this won't be the case?*

Gummo: We are in an era when implementing, or refusing to implement, public policy on the basis of unfounded and archaic stereotypes is not acceptable. We have abandoned this old tendency in many areas of public policy. Now our modern sensibility, which has been fundamental to much social progress, should be brought to our discussion of BIG. Evidence consistently confirms that a BIG program does not automatically bring with it a disincentive to work.

Conversely, we need to critically examine our existing programs which do, intentionally or not, through their claw-back and loss of related benefits provisions create a disincentive to work. Furthermore, evidence from our existing programs consistently confirms a very low rate of 'gaming the system' involving relatively small amounts of money. When we talk about BIG we are talking about a basic level of income. Most people will want more, and be prepared to work for it, because that's the way real people are.

Benns: *What would our communities be like after 10 years of a BIG in place? What changes could you see taking place after a decade of this policy?*

Gummo: Once we have a BIG program up and running for a decade we will observe a society that is more cohesive, healthier, better educated, better housed, more mobile and more mature. To adopt a widely-used contemporary notion, we will have a society that is economically and culturally more sustainable, that has a better chance of flourishing in the long term. We will have new tools to deal more effectively with the challenges of marginalization, alienation, and exclusion, all of which thrive in an environment of inequality.

The economy will operate more consistently because incomes and spending power will be more evenly distributed. Long term investment, for example in tangibles like housing and intangibles like personal actualization, will become more feasible and more secure. People will have a better opportunity to fulfil their ambitions, whatever they may be, and to manifest their creativity. Anything in addition is agreeable detail.

Because it's 2016: Canada could lead the way by pioneering basic income

January 4, 2016

By Roderick Benns

It's a dubious milestone, but one we must acknowledge. According to Oxfam, this is the year in which the wealthiest one percent will surpass the combined wealth of the rest of the world. And because it's 2016, perhaps we should wish to do something about that.

What can Canada do, a country with only .50 percent of the world's population?

It can lead by example. Despite our smaller population, we are a G7 nation with a $2 trillion economy, a respected middle power, and a nation with a long history of social innovation, from Medicare, to Child Tax Credits, to the Registered Disability Savings Plan.

In 2016, to combat growing inequality, Canada can acknowledge that for our capitalist system to work fairly and effectively, the workers who are invested in, and partially responsible for, a company's success have a right to a fair wage. The government could pressure companies through both carrot and stick approaches to ensure more wage and benefits fairness. Decent work, as they say.

Canada could also acknowledge that with the rise of automation and the concomitant rise of precarious work – work that is part time, with no benefits, or of a temporary nature — there is simply not ever again going to be enough decent work to go around. We therefore need to focus on the wellbeing of our citizens. If we do not, our health outcomes suffer, our social cohesion deteriorates, and the overall quality of our lives depreciates.

The best first step we could take is to institute a basic income guarantee. A basic income guarantee ensures everyone an income that is sufficient to meet one's basic needs, regardless of work status. It would be available to all working-age Canadians, when needed, and unlike punitive welfare systems it would not require a person to be completely impoverished to qualify. The net value of the basic income would decline with rising levels of income. It would simply ensure no one slips below the poverty line.

It's the society, stupid

As a colleague recently reminded me, we have become quite accustomed now to hearing and understanding everything through the lens of the economy, rather than through the lens of society. The economy is a subset of society, not the other way around. To alter former U.S President Bill Clinton's famous campaign phrase, 'It's the society, stupid.'

I want to live in a nation that is invested in the creation of a strong, innovative, and just society, of which a healthy economy is an integral aspect.

So as the one percent of the world reach their milestone, Canada should reach for its own milestone and implement a basic income guarantee for all citizens. We will pay for it by ridding ourselves of massive welfare bureaucracies and by eliminating boutique tax credits. Ultimately, we will save more money than we spend by creating a healthier society, since we know poor people have the worst health outcomes and access costly, downstream health services more often than others.

Canada can always choose to do more, as Prime Minister Justin Trudeau is fond of saying. We know what we need to do to create a fair and equitable society. The only question that remains is how we feel about the fact that we haven't yet done so.

One of Canada's top educators, Avis Glaze, says it's time to support basic income

January 6, 2016

By Roderick Benns

One of Canada's foremost educators and an international leader in the field of education, Dr. Avis Glaze, says it's time Canada adopted a basic income guarantee policy.

Glaze — Ontario's first Chief Student Achievement Officer and founding CEO of the Literacy and Numeracy Secretariat — says Canada must address the issue of poverty by addressing the challenge at its source — income.

"To ensure students' life chances are not truncated because of poverty, for me, as an educator, it's absolutely essential that public policy addresses the issue of parental income," Glaze tells *Leaders and Legacies*.

She says she often thinks of the well-known quote from social justice thinker, R. W. Connell: "Statistically speaking, the best advice I would give to a poor child eager to get ahead in education is to choose richer parents."

Glaze, who pioneered character education among other education innovations in Canada, says if we want to ensure Canada is a tapestry of safe and healthy places to live, work and raise our children, "then we must address poverty in a systematic and intentional manner."

"A basic income would be essential if we want to close achievement gaps," says Glaze. "From an educational perspective, this seems to be one of the most intractable issues in education, not only in Canada, but internationally."

Now head of her own consulting company, Edu-quest International Inc., Glaze says she has always believed that educators do meaningful work. "Ultimately, they contribute to nation building."

To that end, she says she has always encouraged her colleagues in education to speak out more about social policy.

"Let's take principals, for example. Many studies show they are a respected group in society. When I speak to them, I ask 'how are you engaging in political action?'"

Glaze says most educators would not describe themselves as 'political.' She says there are many reasons for this. Many do not speak directly to media, since they have trustees and communications departments who speak for the school district.

"But if we think about politics as the ability to influence decision making and to enhance life chances of our students, we must become more political, seeking every opportunity to bend the ears of politicians."

Glaze, as Ontario's first Chief Student Achievement Officer and founding CEO of the Literacy and Numeracy Secretariat, played a pivotal role in improving student achievement in Ontario schools.

She says that regardless of what people say about education from a general perspective, they tend to like their local school and their local principals and teachers. So it's incumbent upon community leaders like them to advocate for social policy change.

Glaze says the spectrum of student needs can't all be left on educators' shoulders.
"While I admire the teachers and principals who are still spending their own money to help their needy students...we need to address the totality of the needs of children as a matter of public policy," Glaze notes.

Long an advocate of business-education partnerships, Glaze says this doesn't mean that schools or school systems should be in the lurch if they don't have the businesses, industries or groups that support their needs, such as breakfast programs.

"And, in any event, these partnerships, though very important, do not address the issue of family incomes," she says.

Glaze says there must be much better integration at the policy level between departments within governments. For instance, education and social policy, or health, economics and education.

"Having silos does not contribute to a problem that is multifaceted in nature. Wherever there are points of natural intersection, we must be prepared to build upon what we have already achieved, and to redouble our efforts to create a multi-pronged, cross-disciplinary focus on the needs of children in general, and those who live in poverty, in particular."

Glaze says Canada can continue to be an example to the world of what it takes to realize one of the promises of its diversity — raising the bar for all children and closing achievement gaps.

"Within the social determinants of health, education and income are perhaps the most powerful," says Glaze. "So addressing the issue of basic income would help tremendously."

Task-paid work instead of real jobs hastens need for basic income, says Kingston woman

January 7, 2016

Roderick Benns recently interviewed Pamela Cornell of Kingston on her involvement with the Basic Income movement.

Benns: *How did you come to be involved in this issue?*

Cornell: While my job affords me healthy exercise and pleasant encounters, it offers little for the mind. The first couple of basic income guarantee meetings I attended in Kingston featured some technical talk about implementation that I found daunting, but I was captivated by the playful exchange of ideas and perspectives. This invigorating group was just what I needed.

The concept of the basic income guarantee appeals to me, both emotionally and intellectually — emotionally, because I remember how stressful it was, being a single parent, struggling to support my daughter and me, in the early seventies. Intellectually, it appeals to me because it's a practical approach to income distribution that will allow our citizens and our society to realize their creative potential.

Benns: *What is your background? Have you ever had lived experience with poverty?*

Cornell: I grew up in the village of Morrisburg, Ontario. My parents were not well-off but, looking back, I don't remember thinking of us as poor, compared to families I knew who lived in shacks with dirt floors. Those were the days when 'tramps' rode the rails, and knocked on doors, offering to cut grass or rake leaves, in exchange for a cheese sandwich.

After graduating from Queen's University, with a degree in English and Philosophy, I worked in London, England, for a year, before returning to Canada, where I thought it would be easier to pay off my student loan. Working as a reporter at *The Peterborough Examiner*, I was sent out to interview the man I would end up marrying. Our daughter was a little over a year old, when my husband came to the realization that he was gay. We separated amicably, but he didn't contribute any financial support for at least four years, and I was too overwhelmed to ask.

I moved to Toronto, where my first apartment was dark, depressing, and overpriced. My daughter and I lived on orange juice, cream of wheat and apples, because that was the most nutritious food I could afford. I found a job writing advertising copy at Sears, but couldn't find day care so had to pay the irritable woman upstairs to look after my daughter, while I was at work. I felt alone and isolated. My social life was non-existent.

At work, the woman who was training me became exasperated because, though I grasped the concepts quickly, I could barely remember anything the following day. Stress was undermining my concentration and short-term memory. I became a night grinder — rapidly wearing down my teeth. I also fell prey to infections — from colds and flu to conjunctivitis (pink eye). I remember waking up with my eyes sealed shut, and having to grope my way to the bathroom to use a warm, wet facecloth to melt that solidified discharge. Fortunately, my employer was patient and, gradually, my circumstances improved.

Benns: *What about basic income policy makes it a smart move for the economy?*

Cornell: For many people, economic hardship is temporary. The causes vary. Divorce or the death of a spouse can mean struggling financially to raise a family on one income. Illness can mean the loss of income, or even of employment. Young people entering the workforce often find themselves in the Catch 22 situation of not being hired, because they lack experience, but then being unable to acquire experience, without a job. A lack of affordable housing can reduce some to sofa surfing.

Moreover, when there isn't enough money to pay for necessities, debt accumulates, adding the cost of interest payments. Energy levels, and health, can be compromised by an inadequate diet. Anxiety levels rise, compromising the immune system. All these factors can serve to prolong the hardship, by undermining people's self-confidence and their health.

The worst of these consequences and their negative effect on productivity could be avoided, or at least reduced, with the assurance a basic income guarantee would provide. It would also eliminate the need for social assistance, with its expensive and demeaning requirement for means testing and intrusive monitoring. It would give entrepreneurs and artists a basic level of security, while they develop — not just their products and creations — but also the networks and markets to sustain their enterprise.

Indications from the Mincome project in Dauphin, Manitoba, are that a basic income guarantee would reduce costly demands on hospitals, policing, and the courts, while increasing people's opportunities to acquire further education and skills-training.

Benns: *What about a basic income guarantee makes it a social justice issue?*

Cornell: Think how unfair is it to be born into poverty and deprived of secure housing and a nutritious diet. How unfair must our society seem to children whose parents are exhausted and ill-tempered from slogging away at several part-time, minimum-wage jobs, while still being unable to meet basic expenses? How fair is it when parental stress causes children to suffer psychological and physical abuse? The economic circumstances of Canadians living in poverty violates

Article 25 of the United Nations' Universal Declaration of Human Rights. A basic income guarantee is an effective way to address that unfairness.

Benns: *The most common concern about implementing a basic income is that too many of us would choose not to work.*

Cornell: The notion that giving people a basic income would turn them into indolent slackers is unfounded. Many already fill every spare moment with unpaid work — for example, looking after young, elderly, or unwell family members; studying; acquiring new skills; and volunteering in the community. People thrive on having a sense of purpose and accomplishment.

A basic income is not a radical notion. It already exists for people over 65, in the form of Old Age Security (OAS) and the Guaranteed Income Supplement (GIS). We simply need to extend it to working-age adults, because our economic reality is changing.

Employers used to offer decent wages, health insurance, paid vacations and defined-benefit pensions. Now jobs like that are in decline. The Uberization of the workforce — where workers are paid by the task — is increasing the precariousness of work. Even people with PhDs face an uncertain future, cobbling together sessional lectureships or consulting contracts. A basic income guarantee would give people income security between periods of employment.

It's time to re-think the idea of paid labour as the requirement for survival. Nobel economics laureate Paul Krugman sees a basic income guarantee as an appropriate response to the increasing share of income going to capital as opposed to labour.

Basic income: The trampoline versus the pit

January 11, 2016

By Roderick Benns

We are told by educators and business leaders today that we need to be nimble for the job market. We are told that in a world with no borders, having an entrepreneurial mindset is the key – a remedy for all the contract work and 'tasks' that now masquerade as jobs. We haven't been told lies — this is all well and true. But we aren't being told the whole truth, either.

The truth is that having such an attitude and stance is not enough. For most, there will be many times when one contract ends and another won't begin seamlessly. A study by the United Way and McMaster University from 2013 shows that only half of the people in the Greater Toronto Area, for example, have standard, full-time jobs. Obviously this means that precarious work is not just for minimum-wage, service-oriented jobs. Precarious work is the new norm for highly-trained technological workers, nursing staff, professors, engineers, and in fact, most professions.

How a Basic Income Would Help

A basic income – ensuring no Canadian would ever drop below the poverty line – would be the best way to protect people from these new realities. Let's say it was set at $20,000 per year. If someone earned $14,000 in one year, then at tax time an additional $6,000 would be given to that person, spread out over 12 months using the existing income tax system. Clean and simple and minimal bureaucracy. No one is overseeing the process to determine if it is 'deserved.' We could scrap the entire welfare system and review other levels of bureaucracy, too.

A basic income would ensure that in between these projects and short-term jobs we provide a trampoline for people to bounce into their next opportunity – rather than the hole or pit that currently exists and is difficult to climb out of, each and every time.

For some, all it would take is two or three rocky months in a row while looking for work to become dangerously impoverished – and our welfare system is the biggest pit of all, where every asset must be liquidated to receive a shockingly small amount of money.

Educators are reacting to the shifting needs of business and are, themselves, trying to do their best to ensure students are ready with relevant skills and knowledge and a capacity for lifelong learning that meets the needs of the marketplace.

But this is an incomplete answer for how to build a society. It illustrates part of the reason, in fact, why education alone cannot solve all social problems. We must also examine how we take care of our people from a social policy standpoint.

Not everyone has the capacity to be entrepreneurial, and all the education in the world will not make them so. That's why we need to set up a basic income guarantee for anyone who needs it. All of us would have access to this minimum standard of living, should we ever have the need.

Fortunately, there are numerous examples from around the world, including Canada, where some form of basic income has been tried.

- In part of Namibia where an unconditional basic income grant was tried, child malnutrition dropped from 42 percent to 10 percent, with close to zero dropouts from school.
- In a World Bank study, researchers gave cash transfers to families in Malawi and ended up increasing school attendance of females with the program because they could afford to go to school to better themselves and their families.

- In eight villages in India, economist Guy Standing reports there was improved housing, better nutrition, better health outcomes, improved school attendance, and more empowerment for those with disabilities.

"Contrary to the skeptics," writes Standing, "the grants led to more labour and work...There was a shift from casual wage labour to more...self-employed farming and business activity, with less distress..."

There will always be people who abuse the system (there are now, in fact) and this will always, thankfully, be a very small percentage. As studies from around the world show, most people are hardwired to do something — to want to make a meaningful contribution of some kind.

As educators work hard to prepare young people to be adaptive and entrepreneurial, our federal and provincial governments should be working hard to adopt this forward-thinking social policy.

We shouldn't have one without the other.

Cornwall City Council endorses Kingston basic income proposal

January 12, 2016

By Roderick Benns

Often called the poorest city in Ontario, the City of Cornwall in eastern Ontario has passed a motion endorsing basic income guarantee policy.

Less than a month ago, the City of Kingston became the first municipality in Canada to call for the development of a basic income guarantee for all Canadians. Its council unanimously passed a motion calling for a national discussion on the issue, hoping this will lead the provinces and federal government to work together to "consider, investigate, and develop a Basic Income Guarantee for all Canadians."

The Kingston resolution was forwarded to all municipalities in Ontario with the request that they consider indicating their own support for the initiative. Cornwall, a city of 46,000, agreed and it was "unanimously passed" according to Cornwall's City Clerk, Helen Finn.

"Council passed it in support of eradicating poverty," Finn tells *Leaders and Legacies.* "Cornwall has a substantial problem with poverty," she adds.

Momentum continues to build for this new shift in social policy, which would ultimately usher in the end of the welfare system and the beginning of a guaranteed income from the government that would keep people above the poverty line.

The policy would ensure everyone an income that is sufficient to meet their basic needs, regardless of work status through direct cash transfers using the income tax system. Finn says that even those who have jobs are not free from poverty. "A large part of the population here are working poor," she says, working for minimum wage and in precarious work that doesn't offer full time hours.

In the motion that passed, Council pointed out a number of converging factors and reasons to support basic income, including income insecurity, precarious employment, inequality, and adverse public health outcomes for people living in poverty. All of which, in turn, can lead to low levels of education, chronic stress, and criminal activity, which is more costly than poverty in the long run.

The case for a basic income guarantee is Canada is growing. Other indicators across Canada that signals growing support for the policy includes:

- The election of an NDP government in Alberta, which was once a Conservative bastion
- Families, Children and Social Development Minister Jean-Yves Duclos, an economist by training, signalled strong support for a basic income guarantee in a 2008 Institute for Research on Public Policy brief, as first published in the Post.
- The election of an Ontario Liberal government that is keen on bold poverty reduction measures
- The support of an increasing number of health-related organizations, such as the Ontario Public Health Association and the Canadian Medical Association.
- The poverty reduction report solicited by the Saskatchewan government and its recommendation to support a basic income policy
- The election of a Liberal government in Prince Edward Island earlier this year that indicated its support for basic income during the campaign

City of Belleville joins Kingston, Cornwall, in municipal push for basic income

January 13, 2016

By Roderick Benns

Calling it "good social policy," Councillor Garnet Thompson has recently sparked the City of Belleville to endorse a basic income guarantee proposal.

Less than a month ago, the City of Kingston became the first municipality in Canada to call for the development of a basic income guarantee for all Canadians. Its council unanimously passed a motion calling for a national discussion on the issue, hoping this will lead the provinces and federal government to work together to "consider, investigate, and develop a Basic Income Guarantee for all Canadians."

The Kingston resolution was forwarded to all municipalities in Ontario with the request that they consider indicating their own support for the initiative. The City of Cornwall has also endorsed the motion.

"I think it's a policy that will help get all levels of government engaged," Thompson tells *Leaders and Legacies*.

Thompson, who brought forward the motion before Belleville City Council, says the kind of work that is often available now isn't meeting the needs of enough people. "It's obvious to me that people can't live on what they're earning," says Thompson, referring to minimum wage jobs that are often not even full time and lack benefits.

He says there's not enough affordable housing in the city, with about 1,400-1,600 people on a waiting list. Those who can't wait are paying market rates on their inadequate wages or social services money, "which isn't sustainable."

Belleville, a relatively prosperous city of 50,000 with a broad economy, nonetheless is on the same trajectory as many other Canadian towns and cities – increasingly at the mercy of precarious work, with more part time jobs, contract positions, and jobs without benefits.

Thompson, who is also a board member of the local Canadian Mental Health Association, says when a parent has to hold down two or three part-time jobs just to make ends meet, "it's a stress on families."

"It affects mental health. The courts are inundated with cases connected to mental health issues and it often has connections to poverty."

Momentum continues to build for this new shift in social policy, which would ultimately usher in the end of the welfare system and the beginning of a guaranteed income from the government that would keep people above the poverty line.

The policy would ensure everyone an income that is sufficient to meet their basic needs, regardless of work status through direct cash transfers using the income tax system.

In the motion that originally passed at Kingston City Council, a number of converging factors and reasons to support basic income were given, including income insecurity, precarious employment, inequality, and adverse public health outcomes for people living in poverty. All of which, in turn, can lead to low levels of education, chronic stress, and criminal activity, which is more costly than poverty in the long run.

Town of Pelham joins the basic income movement, endorses Kingston motion

January 14, 2016

By Roderick Benns

In the town where Canada's largest sugar maple tree grows, the local town council hopes the growth of a movement will benefit its own people along the way, too.

The Town of Pelham, Ontario, is a rural-urban mix of communities in the heart of the Niagara Region. Council passed a motion this week endorsing a Kingston resolution calling for the provinces and federal government to work together to "consider, investigate, and develop a Basic Income Guarantee for all Canadians."

The Kingston resolution was forwarded to all municipalities in Ontario with the request that they consider indicating their own support for the initiative.

Councillor John Durley, who made the motion, notes that in addition to helping those living in poverty, a basic income would be "great for the economy."

"We have a large senior's population, and they tend to be most in need here," he says. He also notes the local food bank seems to be busy, a sign of a precarious economy where job prospects aren't always certain. He estimates about 15 percent of the population lives in poverty.

"We're an above-average area in terms of wages," Durley notes, "but not everyone has access to those jobs."

Momentum continues to build for this potential new shift in social policy, which would ultimately usher in the end of the welfare system and the beginning of a guaranteed income from the government that would keep people above the poverty line.

The policy would ensure everyone an income that is sufficient to meet their basic needs, regardless of work status, through direct cash transfers using the income tax system.

In the motion that originally passed at Kingston City Council, a number of converging factors and reasons to support basic income were given, including income insecurity, precarious employment, inequality, and adverse public health outcomes for people living in poverty.

All of which, in turn, can lead to low levels of education, chronic stress, and criminal activity, which is more costly than poverty in the long run.

Potatoes and Poverty: Basic income, not Band-Aids, is needed says retired professor

January 15, 2016

By Roderick Benns

In the mid 1960s, a young, untrained social worker named Roberta Hamilton was given the task of visiting families in Leeds County on behalf of the Children's Aid Society. The rural Ontario poverty she encountered more than 50 years ago was devastating.

Some families had only potatoes for dinner. Many couldn't find work. Farming on the rocky hills and outcrops of the region ensured the harvest was scarce. With the exception of a cheese factory in Plum Hollow, industry was scarcer still.

Procuring welfare for these desperately poor people was difficult. At the time, says Hamilton, "it was the reeve of the township that decided whether a family should get the pittance or not."

"I witnessed the humiliation of my clients who had to beg for the most basic necessities — and I begged on their behalf," she says. As well, I "often bought groceries for a destitute family."

For the hard-working farmers of the county, says Hamilton, who were also trying to manage their own small crops, the notion of welfare rubbed them the wrong way.

"Providing welfare was like giving their own hard-earned cash to their 'dissolute' neighbours," she tells *Leaders and Legacies*.

Hamilton says the housekeeper of one reeve told her that sanitary napkins were a luxury that poor people should not buy. It was during this time that Hamilton realized that poverty was a problem "not to be solved by social workers with a bag full of Band-Aids."

That year marked her strong commitment to democratic socialism, a commitment that has not wavered since. She followed the recommendations of the landmark David Croll report from the Senate Committee on Poverty closely. She became convinced about the importance of a Guaranteed Annual Income.

"Everyone, I decided, should be entitled to a decent living, no matter the circumstances of their life," she says.

Hamilton went on to become a sociology professor and taught at at Queen's University in Kingston for 25 years, where she still resides today. When she retired, she turned her attention away from university politics and towards something bigger — the vision of securing a basic income guarantee for Canadians.

She says it's easier for people to wrap their minds around the idea and give support to the notion of a living wage instead of basic income, "because we are so wedded to the idea that people who don't have paid employment are parasites and lazy."

They believe that work "is the ticket for all life's material goods and needs from housing to food to education."

"There are many reasons to challenge this view," the retired professor notes, including the fact that any society "that purports to be interested in social equality and the worth of all human beings needs to distribute resources fairly."

"A good society needs to distribute income to everyone — those raising children, people with a disability, artists and musicians, young people looking to find some sort of berth in the economy, those with mental health problems...the list goes on," she says.

Hamilton says the biggest roadblock to mentally accepting the idea of a basic income guarantee is the fact that most people assume everyone would stop working.

"But when you ask people who think this if they would stop working if they had a basic income, they look at you as if you were crazy. It's only those 'other' people who would choose not to work."

She says in her experience, those 'others' are few and far between, and even those few who might choose not to work don't make a lifetime habit of this.

"Perhaps some people would reject jobs that provide wages below the poverty line, miserable conditions, and no benefits. So employers would have to rethink their employment strategies. What a good thing that would be."

City of Welland backs Kingston motion

January 22, 2016

By Roderick Benns

Ontario's City of Welland, about a half hour away from Niagara Falls, is backing Kingston's basic income guarantee motion.

Led by Councillor Bonnie Fokkens, Council unanimously supported the motion calling for a national discussion on the issue, urging the provinces and federal government to work together to "consider, investigate, and develop a Basic Income Guarantee for all Canadians."

Momentum continues to build for this new shift in social policy, which would ultimately usher in the end of the welfare system and the beginning of a guaranteed income from the government that would keep people above the poverty line.

The policy would ensure everyone an income that is sufficient to meet their basic needs, regardless of work status through direct cash transfers using the income tax system. Essentially, a basic income would ensure that no Canadian would ever drop below the poverty line.

Welland, a city of 51,000, is one of many municipalities speaking out in favour of the need for this social policy shift. The Kingston resolution was forwarded to all municipalities in Ontario with the request that they consider indicating their own support for the initiative. It was also forwarded to the Association of Municipalities of Ontario and the Federation of Canadian Municipalities.

A Basic Income Guarantee and its value to employed people

January 25, 2016

By Roderick Benns

A basic income should be Canada's next great social program. Even if you are a fully employed person, there are many reasons to support a basic income guarantee. We'll talk about just three of them below.

But first, what is a basic income guarantee?

A basic income would ensure that no Canadian would ever drop below the poverty line. Let's say it was set at $20,000 per year. If someone earned $15,000 in one year, then at tax time an additional $5,000 would be given to that person, spread out over 12 months using the existing income tax system. Clean and simple and minimal bureaucracy. No one is overseeing the process to determine if it is 'deserved.' We could scrap the entire welfare system and review other levels of bureaucracy, too.

In addition to the bureaucracy savings, Canada already spends up to $86 billion a year in combatting poverty...and yet we still have poverty. Basic income is simple in design and effective. No one gets left behind.

Now, on to those top three reasons...

Top three reasons for the fully employed to support Basic Income

1. It's not the 1950s anymore and jobs aren't guaranteed for life. Just because you're working now, it might only take an economic downturn or a corporate restructuring and anyone — including you — could be out of work. If a basic income

policy were in place, you would be assured of enough money to keep you above the poverty while you are searching for new opportunities. Think of basic income as a trampoline that helps you bounce into a new opportunity. With welfare, you would have to liquidate every asset you have just to qualify for money that isn't even enough to live on.

2. Having a basic income guarantee will actually create better jobs. This will happen because employers will have to offer fair compensation to you. If they don't, you as an employee can refuse the work for the pay being offered because you know you won't be in desperation mode. The basic income guarantee is your back-up. While very few people would want to live on just a basic income guarantee for long, this will help tip the scales back toward employees.

3. Work is far more precarious today, with more people employed part-time, doing contract work, and often without benefits. Having a basic income guarantee would ensure you don't slip into poverty while looking for new prospects.

City of Peterborough councillor ready to adopt basic income motion

February 3, 2016

By Roderick Benns

As the City of Peterborough considers whether to support a basic income guarantee, at least one councillor is ready to offer her support right now.

Councillor Diane Therrien, known for her support of many social justice issues, is also the facilitator of community education and engagement with the Peterborough Poverty Reduction Network.

"I'm happy to support basic income policy," she tells *Leaders and Legacies*. "I think it's an idea that is long overdue."

The City of Kingston became the first municipality in Canada to call for the development of a basic income guarantee for all Canadians. Its council unanimously passed a motion calling for a national discussion on the issue, hoping this will lead the provinces and federal government to work together to "consider, investigate, and develop a Basic Income Guarantee for all Canadians."

The resolution was forwarded to all municipalities in Ontario with the request that they consider indicating their own support for the initiative. While the County of Peterborough has already shown its support for the Kingston motion, Therrien says some councillors at the City level want more background information on the topic since some were not familiar with it.

A basic income would ensure that no Canadian would ever drop below the poverty line. In one of the most common models, a basic income threshold is established – say, $20,000 per year per person.

If someone earned $15,000 in one year, then at tax time an additional $5,000 would be given to that person, spread out over 12 months using the existing income tax system. Most people feel this would allow governments to scrap the entire welfare system and review other levels of bureaucracy, too.

"It evens the playing field," points out Therrien. "There are so many positive cost savings from a basic income approach, especially in social services and health care."

In the motion that originally passed at Kingston City Council, a number of reasons to support basic income were given, including income insecurity, precarious employment, inequality, and adverse public health outcomes for people living in poverty.

"A lot of people think this is radical, but it's really not," says Therrien. "There are many examples of where this has been tried" around the world.

In fact, there are current pilot projects being set up in the Netherlands and in Finland. As well:

- In part of Namibia where an unconditional basic income grant was tried, child malnutrition dropped from 42 percent to 10 per cent, with close to zero dropouts from school.
- In a World Bank study, researchers gave cash transfers to families in Malawi and ended up increasing school attendance of females because they could afford to go to school to better themselves and their families.
- In eight villages in India, economist Guy Standing reports there was improved housing, better nutrition, better health outcomes, improved school attendance, and more empowerment for those with disabilities.

City of Peterborough council will most likely vote on this issue in three to six weeks time, according to Therrien.

President of AMO, Tecumseh mayor, says time to be bold and support basic income

February 5, 2016

By Roderick Benns

The mayor of Tecumseh, Ontario, who also serves as president of the Association of Municipalities Ontario (AMO), says it's time to be bold and fight poverty with a basic income guarantee, not continue to "tinker at the edges."

Mayor Gary McNamara, who recently led Tecumseh Town Council to support a basic income guarantee motion, says he is glad to see so much support for the policy happening across all three levels of government. This includes recent comments from Jean-Yves Duclos, the Minister for families, children and social development, who is looking at a basic income guarantee from a federal perspective, and Francois Blais in Quebec who has been asked to investigate the policy for Quebec Premier Phillipe Couillard.

The basic income motion supported by Tecumseh has its origins in Kingston, Ontario. Its council unanimously passed a motion calling for a national discussion on the issue, hoping this would lead the provinces and federal government to work together to "consider, investigate, and develop a Basic Income Guarantee for all Canadians."

The Kingston resolution was forwarded to all municipalities in Ontario with the request that they consider indicating their own support for the initiative, which Tecumseh has done.

"It's getting some great traction," McNamara tells *Leaders and Legacies*.

He says it has also been discussed at the AMO level, where communities range in size from 173 to just under one million.

"We all want to figure out how we get ourselves in a position where every Canadian has a basic living amount...and if this is to be successful, we need all three levels of government to make it happen," says the mayor.

McNamara says the policy people at AMO are busy researching the issue, "to approach it in a sensible and sustainable way."

The mayor says Kingston has created a "foundational piece" at the municipal level and that it's "growing."

"The good news is, it appears to have gotten to the (federal) minister's desk.

McNamara says he has spent his last two terms as mayor wondering thinking more about how to help "the working poor" and those who are fully dependent on social services.

The mayor says he has spent 25 years in municipal politics and has been blessed with a good life. But even looking at the costs he has faced over the years, including his own kids' post-secondary education costs, he wonders how families with only one or two minimum wage jobs can get by.

"I'm saying to myself, how the heck did these people survive? How do we get over the hump to create more opportunities for people?"

McNamara says he's "just a small town mayor."

"But I know when you want real change you have to be bold. I don't think we can just tinker at the edges of social policy anymore."

Timid choice for City of Kawartha Lakes to back out of basic income discussion

February 8, 2016

By Roderick Benns

We recently learned that the City of Kawartha Lakes isn't big on having conversations.

How else to explain their reluctance to pass a simple motion sent to all municipalities in Ontario from the City of Kingston, asking that they endorse having a national conversation about a basic income guarantee for Canadians?

A basic income guarantee is known by many names, including a guaranteed annual income and negative income tax. But the essence is that it ensures everyone an income sufficient to meet their basic needs, regardless of work status.

Let's say it was set at $18,000 per year. If someone earned $12,000 in one year at a part-time job, then at tax time an additional $6,000 would be given to that person, spread out over 12 months using the existing income tax system. Clean and simple and minimal bureaucracy. With basic income, no one is overseeing the process to determine if it is 'deserved.' We could literally scrap the entire welfare system and review other levels of bureaucracy for savings, too.

According to *Kawartha Lakes This Week*, most councillors were against getting involved. Councillor Pat Dunn is quoted as saying, "I can guarantee it's going to come out of taxpayers' [pockets]." "This is ridiculous; it is so far out of our mandate..."

I do wonder when we all started becoming 'taxpayers' and stopped being citizens. When did we start focusing only on what's best for the economy and not what's best for society? A good economy is under the umbrella of a good society, not the other way around.

At least two councillors objected to Coun. Dunn's comments. Both Councillors Doug Elsmlie and Patrick O'Reilly indicated that supporting the motion would merely signal an opportunity to engage the Province and federal government, who would obviously be the funders.

Nearby, Peterborough County Council endorsed the Kingston motion. The City of Peterborough is still considering it. They saw the value of having a conversation about an issue that would affect the lives of all their citizens in one way or another, not just low-income earners.

In the downstream effects of poverty, though, it is towns and cities – the level of government closest to the people – that sees the effect of poverty firsthand. So why the reluctance to have a conversation in the City of Kawartha Lakes?

These are good conversations to have. It is unfortunate the City of Kawartha Lakes has chosen to remain dumb on this issue.

Manitoba farm family's 'Mincome truck' a symbol of common sense for basic income advocate

February 12, 2016

By Roderick Benns

The best story Ron Hikel ever heard about the famous 'Mincome' experiment from the 1970s has to do with a simple pick-up truck.

Mincome stands for minimum income — something that was given to about a third of the people who lived in Dauphin, Manitoba. It was a bold experiment started by the federal Liberal government to see what people would do with free money from the state.

Ron Hikel was the executive director of the Mincome project, a program that ran from from 1974 through 1978. When a Dutch TV crew showed up at his doorstep last year in Toronto to talk to him about Mincome, they then went on to Dauphin where the experiment had made everyone in the town eligible to apply for monthly income supplementation, based on earned income and family size.

Hikel says they found and filmed a local farming family who, according to the surviving mother and son, Clarke Williams, told the film crew an interesting story. Back in the mid-70s, the family relied on two old trucks but badly needed a new one.

"So the mother put aside enough of the monthly Mincome money," Hikel tells *Leaders and Legacies*, "to make the down payment on a new truck."

Hikel says the family didn't have to sell off any of the precious livestock they owned and relied upon for income. The new truck was purchased before the end of the Mincome experiment and the family ran the vehicle for 25 straight years.

In the film, Clarke leads the documentary makers out into a field and shows them the old blue GMC truck, with a battery still in it, sitting quietly there to this day. Hikel says he thinks of this vehicle as the 'Mincome truck,' an example of the "productively invested use of the Mincome money to sustain a family's livelihood and independence, for more than two decades."

Though Mincome ended prematurely in the late 1970s, momentum continues to build to create some form of basic income guarantee for Canadians to ensure that no one would ever drop below the poverty line. This would ultimately usher in the end of the welfare system.

Top Mincome director says Canadian basic income advocates should act fast

February 16, 2016

Roderick Benns recently interviewed Ron Hikel, the executive director of the well-known Mincome project in Dauphin, Manitoba. It was a program that ran from from 1974 through 1978 which helped establish a minimum income for about a third of the people who lived there. Hikel was also the former deputy minister of health in Manitoba, and was deputy chief of staff to a US Congressman, working on Capitol Hill in the first two years of Barack Obama's administration.

Benns: *What are two or three big take-aways about basic income policy that Mincome taught you?*

Hikel: The biggest single take-away is that whatever a government decides to do, or not do, depends very much on their political evaluation of the policy environment prevailing at any given moment; and that this context can change very quickly. It can go from favourable to neutral to hostile in a short time. Unfortunately, controlled social science experiments take years, if they are done properly, and in that time, the policy atmosphere will most certainly change.

This can make the once-possible, unimaginable and the previously unimaginable quite attractive. That is both what happened to Mincome when the governments decided not to analyze the data, and also explains why more than 40 years later, the concept has cycled back into fashion. I cannot guess how long this new phase will last, but those who believe in the idea should be acting quickly.

Benns: *What gives you great optimism about the basic income movement in Canada right now?*

Hikel: I fear I have spent too many years in and around governments to be awash in the warm glow of expectation. Rather, I do see several new social and economic factors that are prompting renewed and widely-spread interest in the concept. One of these is the precariousness of new job creation paying enough to live decently on, resulting from great technological innovation and globalization, given the associated job destruction here in Canada and re-location elsewhere. Also, the movement is now international, prompting, in response, consideration of various forms of basic income in at least half a dozen nations. This in turn legitimizes Canadian government interest. But I would not yet confuse that interest with a firm decision to act.

Benns: *Do you have a preference – universal demogrant or more like the negative income tax model which would be universally available in times of need? Why?*

Hikel: As to a favoured form of basic income design, that is best left up to governments to decide, based on their policy objectives, their sense of the public interest, the size of the available spend and the extent to which any new program is used to consolidate or integrate it with existing income support programs. I believe in that old adage 'perfection can be the enemy of progress.' A modest program, once introduced and improved by experience over time, can be safely made more generous later.

Benns: *One of the biggest concerns heard about basic income is that people will choose not to work. Is there a justifiable fear that soon there won't be anyone to do the more unsavoury jobs out there?*

Hikel: As to the legitimacy of the fear of reducing work incentives, the experiments of the 1970s show varying results. That concern can be largely anticipated and mitigated by finding the right program design, combined with effective operating rules, for a particular province, region, or nation. As well, differing provincial demographic and economic factors need to be considered here. The same thing applies to avoiding adverse effects on wage rates and employment. Some of those matters are best left to economists, in consultation with business leaders, unions and community leaders.

Ontario government to try basic income guarantee pilot

February 26, 2016

By Roderick Benns

After a groundswell of support from mayors across the province, including pressure from health units and organizations of all social policy stripes, Ontario will proceed with a basic income guarantee pilot project.

The location of the pilot has not yet been announced but the recent provincial budget document makes clear that the government pledges to "work with communities, researchers and other stakeholders in 2016 to determine how best to design and implement a Basic Income pilot."

A basic income can take different forms but it is generally understood to ensure everyone an income that is sufficient to meet their basic needs, regardless of work status.

The budget also states that, "The pilot project will test a growing view at home and abroad that a basic income could build on the success of minimum wage policies and increases in child benefits by providing more consistent and predictable support in the context of today's dynamic labour market."

Further, the budget notes that "the pilot would also test whether a basic income would provide a more efficient way of delivering income support, strengthen the attachment to the labour force, and achieve savings in other areas, such as health care and housing supports."

Prior to this, *Leaders and Legacies* helped place the issue on the municipal agenda by interviewing mayors across Canada.

Calgary's Mayor Naheed Nenshi and Edmonton's Mayor Don Iveson galvanized discussion on this issue. They were soon joined by Halifax's Mike Savage and St. John's Mayor Dennis O'Keefe. In fact, no less than nine provincial and territorial capital leaders support basic income or at least pilot projects. Innumerable smaller city and town mayors across the nation — many of them in Ontario — also declared their support as well.

Dr. Evelyn Forget, who is one of Canada's top researchers on basic income, was a key influencer of the Ontario government's decision to try a pilot, along with Mincome executive director Ron Hikel. Mincome was the experiment tried in the 1970s in Dauphin, Manitoba, and it was Dr. Forget who found this data and analyzed it. Her analysis of Dauphin's basic income experiment is held up around the world as promising data and a reason to move forward with basic income social policy.

After the Ontario budget's announcement, Dr. Forget tells *Leaders and Legacies* and the Basic Income Canada Network (BICN) that timing is everything.

"Sometimes all the forces in the universe align. It's time. Nothing can stop an idea whose time has come," Dr. Forget says.

The chair of BICN, Sheila Regehr, says "kudos to Ontario for its vision and the opportunity to roll up our sleeves to design the basic income we want and need."

"We need it rolled out across Canada, and Quebec too is in the game, so there's no reason why people and governments in other parts of this country need sit on the sidelines — it's time for us all to get to work," Regehr says.

Senator Art Eggleton calls on federal government to launch Basic Income pilot

February 26, 2016

By Roderick Benns

Long-time anti-poverty crusader, Senator Art Eggleton, has just called on the federal government to launch a basic income pilot project with the cooperation of one or more provinces and territories. Eggleton tabled the motion from the Senate today, calling for a basic income model "for the purpose of helping Canadians to escape poverty."

According to a 2013 poll done by Environics the basic income is supported by a majority of Canadians and across the political spectrum including many federal, provincial and municipal leaders.

"The time is right to test a basic income" says Eggleton. "How we have dealt with poverty has failed. Instead of lifting people out of poverty our current programs entrap them. We need to test a different approach."

A basic income, through a negative income tax, would be administered through the tax system where if someone's income is less than the poverty line they would simply be topped up over the poverty line.

In a January, 2015 interview with *Leaders and Legacies*, Eggleton said then that "in order to build political will we need a contemporary pilot project, and I'm hopeful that's what we can do."

Eggleton noted then that a pilot project would be the best way to dispel concerns that people will give up working if their basic needs are met. A basic income guarantee, he said, "isn't the good life, it's the basics."

"The vast majority of people want to do more than that. We use up enormous resources of thought examining whether or not people will stop working if we ensure they aren't in poverty. This just isn't true. Our worry that people are going to laze around and not get jobs is ludicrous," Eggleton said at the time.

Recently Jean-Yves Duclos, federal Minister of Families, Children and Social Development, stated that a guaranteed minimum income is a policy with merit for discussion. At the same time, Francois Blais, Minister of Employment and Social Solidarity in Quebec, has been asked by Premier Phillipe Couillard to figure out how the province might turn their existing income support tools in the direction of a basic income guarantee.

Yesterday, the Ontario government announced it would fund a basic income guarantee pilot in an undisclosed location. From the Senate today, Eggleton was hopeful for what could this mean for people living in poverty.

"Poverty costs us all. It expands health-care costs, policing burdens, and depresses the economy" says Eggleton.

"If proven effective a basic income would not only end poverty but we would spend smarter, more efficiently and effectively."

With stability through Basic Income, most will choose to work: Debra McAuslan

February 22, 2016

Roderick Benns recently interviewed Debra McAuslan, who advocates for basic income through her affiliation with the Kingston Basic Income group.

Benns: *How did you come to be involved with the fight for a Basic Income?*

McAuslan: I had heard about basic income policy almost 30 years ago, but did not understand poverty. I grew up on a farm in southwestern Ontario. I must say I have never personally known poverty. Naively, as a young adult, I believed everyone must have had the same experience I had. In nursing school during my psychiatry rotation I was totally overwhelmed by the prevalence of sexual abuse in the patient histories.

During my nursing career, seeing those living in poverty (when I had the privilege of visiting people's homes during my years as a VON nurse) helped me to see the impact of poverty on health and the challenges of rural poverty.

In my 30s, within one year, my mother was diagnosed with cancer, my second child was born and my marriage fell apart. It was a dark time in my life. I was working part time and could not afford the mortgage in the city, so moved back to the rural community I grew up in with my two children. I had a good paying job, had financial security, and a loving family that helped me with child care and emotional support. I made it through those tough years, raising children on my own, the death of my mother and the struggle to get further education. I have always wondered how someone without all the supports I had makes it through life's challenges.

In the last few years I have gotten to know several people living in poverty through my church. Their experiences of the system, the challenges obtaining food for their children, the overwhelming paperwork, the multitude of agencies that do not communicate with each other and the judgement they face has been an education for me. I knew something had to be done. I found the Kingston Basic Income Facebook site one day and called them to volunteer my help.

Benns: *What about basic income policy makes it a smart move for the economy?*

McAuslan: Currently one in seven or 4.9 million Canadians live below the poverty line and struggle with the insecurity of shelter, food and other basic needs. Some qualify for social assistance, a system that provides inadequate monies and is laden with disincentives to work and continual judgment. There are also the working poor struggling for enough money for the same needs as well as day care. Getting ahead seems like an impossible dream.

We are often overwhelmed with the multitude of requests for charitable dollars. This reflects an attempt to fill the gaps of poverty. It is estimated that the cost of homelessness in Canada is $4.9 billion per year. We know that poverty and health are linked. The tax payer cost to our health care system specifically due to poverty is estimated to be $7.6 billion per year. We know that there is a link between poverty and the criminal justice system. The savings in dismantling the infrastructure, in health care and the criminal justice systems would be substantial.

Food Banks, United Way, the Salvation Army and other churches and charities help provide food and support both emotionally and financially...but doesn't come close to meeting the need.

A Basic Income Guarantee would provide financial security for all people, to know there is a cheque coming that will keep them above the poverty line and that they can work and get ahead without penalty.

Benns: *Why do you think a 'living wage' gets more press than basic income?*

McAuslan: A living wage is commendable, but will only help those who are employed. The assumption that all people are able to work full time is erroneous. For many, whether it be from mental health issues, learning disabilities, and so on, obtaining and/or keeping a full time job is impossible. Sometimes this is a temporary time in their lives, where they just need some stability to get on their feet again. For others this will be a life-long struggle.

Benns: *The most common concern is about implementing a basic income guarantee is that too many of us would choose not to work. Why do you believe this won't be the case?*

McAuslan: Dr. Evelyn Forget's analysis of the data from the Dauphin, Manitoba's Mincome experiment in the 1970s showed that people did continue to work with the exception of two groups. One group was young mothers (before the one year pregnancy leave was initiated) and the other was teenagers. Another finding was that teenagers spent more time in school and more graduated.

A single mother I have met would like to return to work now that her children are in school. Any income she makes will be deducted from her next month's social assistance cheque. She told me she will lose dental and drug benefits for her children if she makes more than $1,000 per month, so she chooses not to work. When people's lives are stable financially and they are healthy, almost all will choose to work.

Building 'social solidarity' with basic income: Elaine Power

February 23, 2016

Roderick Benns recently interviewed Elaine Power, an associate professor in the School of Kinesiology and Health Studies at Queen's University in Kingston, about the need for a Basic Income Guarantee in Canada.

Benns: *What about a basic income guarantee makes it a social justice issue?*

Power: Our economic system creates poverty and creates competition for scarce resources, including paid employment. Even though there is lots of work to be done, and lots of money in our economy, there are not enough paid jobs for everyone who needs or wants one. And there is lots of work that is very worthwhile but that no private employer will pay for, such as cleaning up natural habitats or waterways.

We are among the wealthiest countries in the world, but that wealth is unevenly and unfairly distributed. Since our economic system creates poverty for some people, then collectively we have a moral and ethical obligation to ensure that everyone can at least meet their basic human needs. A basic income would provide a material foundation to give people the freedom to decide how to best live their lives and how to best contribute to society. In other words, basic income helps ensure positive liberty.

Canada has signed multiple international agreement and covenants declaring that we believe everyone has a right to the basics of life. For example article 25 of the Universal Declaration of Human Rights, to which Canada is a signatory, states:

Everyone has the right to a standard of living adequate for the health and well-being of himself [sic] and of his [sic] family, including food, clothing, housing and medical care and necessary social services, and the right to security in the event of unemployment, sickness, disability, widowhood, old age or other lack of livelihood in circumstances beyond his control.

On the international stage, we like to present ourselves as being on board with the idea of ensuring that everyone can meet basic human needs. Why haven't we been able to hold our governments to account for this?

Benns: *The most common concern about implementing a basic income guarantee is that too many of us would choose not to work. Why do you believe this won't be the case?*

Power: We work for lots of different reasons, not just money. And most of us do work that is never paid. To start, we need to change our ideas about work, not just counting the activities that get paid. For many of us, the most meaningful activities in our lives are unpaid. Maybe more of us would chose to spend our time doing more meaningful activities when a basic income is implemented. Basic income will never provide a luxurious standard of living.

Most people would chose to have paid employment for all its benefits, including monetary benefits, to have a better standard of living. Moreover, I think a basic income could help us shift the ethos of our times, which is about grabbing as much as we can for ourselves without regard for others or for the common good. I think we rise (or descend) to the expectations put upon us. If we set up expectations that everyone has something to contribute to the common good, I think ordinary people would rise to these expectations. While there has been much fear-mongering and divisiveness in recent political discourse, our new federal government seems intent to appeal to the "better angels of our nature." I think a basic income could reinforce this and encourage us all to do the work that we are able to do to make the world a better place.

Research from all over the world, including the Canadian MINCOME experiment, shows no work disincentive from a basic income. In recent studies in lower income countries, basic income actually gives people a springboard into paid employment.

Benns: *When you imagine Canadian life with this policy in place — say 10 or 20 years of a basic income guarantee — what does the country look like? How has it changed?*

Power: We have been so conditioned to think about the bottom line on every issue that we have forgotten to imagine what kind of country we want to create together. Goodness – Canada without poverty! I think about the liberation of human potential and the end of needless suffering from deprivation. I think about all the energy and talents that will be available to tackle other issues, like climate change and social isolation. I think about people being able to attend to their own healing, such as addictions and trauma, so that they and their children can live in more inner peace, which will translate into more outer peace in our world.

In her latest book, *This Changes Everything*, Naomi Klein advocates a basic income to help break the stranglehold that the current political ethos has on our collective imagination — the competitive individualism that separates us from each other and tells us we are on our own to grab what we can. Basic income would help us rebuild a sense of social solidarity. I think a basic income will lessen depression, anxiety and other forms of mental illness that our insecure, unstable and competitive world induces. It will help us to draw out the best of ourselves and each other. I hope we will become a more compassionate, caring and just society. It will take more than 10 or 20 years but basic income is essential to creating "the more beautiful world our hearts know is possible."

Decide now on what results are acceptable from basic income pilots, says PhD candidate

March 17, 2016

Roderick Benns recently interviewed David Calnitsky, who is a Canadian PhD candidate in Sociology at the University of Wisconsin-Madison, completing his thesis on the Mincome experiment with basic income. The experiment took place in the 1970s in Dauphin, Manitoba. He has recently published part of it as an article: "More Normal than Welfare: The Mincome Experiment, Stigma, and Community Experience."

Benns: *What were two or three of the most revealing aspects of the Dauphin, MB experiment with basic income, in terms of how it changed people's lives?*

Calnitsky: My recent paper is on social stigma, and broadly, the "dignity problem," which I think gets insufficient attention in these debates. Participants with experience in the welfare system wrote about the pervasive indignities inflicted on them. Meanwhile, when asked about Mincome, people viewed the program as a pragmatic source of assistance. According to people's accounts, participating in Mincome didn't damage your standing in the community.

And there's a couple reasons for that. First, instead of degrading and invasive case-worker discretion, Mincome was not unlike the un-stigmatizing benefits that can come at tax time. It didn't have the same case-by-case treatment, the searching investigation of recipients' lives. The whole thing could be done by mail. And second, perhaps more importantly, it was a broadly available, universalistic program. It treated lots of different people in a similar manner. It blurred the lines of demarcation between low-wage workers, the disabled, unemployed workers, and former social assistance recipients. The more universalistic a program, the more people it reaches, the more normal it starts to feel.

So, for example, one person wrote, "I feel that [welfare] is more for disabled or people which are too lazy to work. It doesn't include us, we're both able and willing to work but can't get a job due to the low employment rate." They joined Mincome simply because they were "short of money." Mincome was less likely to signal your moral worth, instead it was just a practical problem solver.

If we're interested in social policies that are resilient I think the dignity problem, or the moral aspects of these policies are worth considering more closely. Universalistic income maintenance programs will be popular, and that popularity is a key source of their sustainability. What's more, unlike targeted welfare programs, they don't exacerbate divisions among poor and working people.

Benns: *We seem to be on the path to more pilot projects in Canada, with updated data. Broadly, do you have a prediction about the results that we will see? Will the changes in society since the 1970s inevitably affect the data?*

Calnitsky: I think pilot projects are extremely exciting. There are, however, some pitfalls to watch out for. From my perspective, looking at the Mincome experiment, one of the problems with the experimental approach is that you get a lot of empirical scrutiny, but you miss the important "popularity" effect. That is, for a basic income advocate, the difference between running an experiment and actually implementing the thing, is that only in the latter do you have the popularity of the policy working on your side, making it difficult for politicians to put the kibosh on things, or politely ignore it in the face of inevitably ambiguous evidence.

Mincome was popular; but popularity can translate into robust social policy only once it's implemented widely. Universal healthcare in Canada was simply implemented. Once in place its popularity made it hard to roll back. If we had experimented with it first, it would be easy to imagine some negative findings coming out here and there, harming its chances of being realized.

This issue is compounded by the fact that it's often not clear what results are acceptable. The debates around US and Canadian experiments from the 1970s were muddled from the outset because there was no prior agreement on what amount of work reduction was acceptable. So, proponents and opponents alike had ammunition: proponents observed the small reductions in work as vindications of the program's feasibility, while opponents interpreted the same data as a sign of the program's failure.

In terms of changes since the 1970s I'd make two points. First, there's no question that there is a gap between a small rural town and contemporary labour markets. In spite of that, the precarity of Dauphin's seasonal labour market bears a certain resemblance to the contemporary world of work. On this score a number of participants said they joined Mincome for security-related reasons. One woman said this: "Uncertain of husband's earning abilities for [the] winter months as seasons sometimes affects his earnings. . . . If one loses a job (or illness) I feel Mincome gives families a little more security and helps remove some extra fears." Her family faced a different set of circumstances, but insecurity is a common thread. And there is little doubt that labour markets are even less secure than they were in the 1970s.

Second, regarding the contemporary welfare system, there have been important changes, but in many ways we see the same regulation of the lives of the poor, the same distinctions between the "deserving" and "undeserving." Recent studies show that the social assistance system continues to be marked by deep social stigmatization, and I think we have every reason to expect that a more universalistic and unconditional system would improve people's lives in much the same way it did in the 1970s.

Benns: *You did qualitative research of the Dauphin years with basic income. Is there a particular story/anecdote that stands out for you for its power?*

Calnitsky: Perhaps what's most interesting is that I found that Mincome's social meaning was powerful enough that even participants who themselves had particularly negative attitudes toward social assistance—people who opposed welfare on moral grounds, who saw welfare recipients in a negative light, and who believed strongly in the principle of earning one's own living—felt able to collect Mincome payments without a sense of contradiction.

A man who wrote, "Welfare to me was accepting something for nothing," joined Mincome because it "would be a benefit to me at some time."

Another person refused welfare, saying "welfare is for (the) needy or bums"; he joined Mincome for pragmatic reasons: "For the extra income."

A third refused welfare saying, "I'm able to support myself." He joined Mincome saying, "I might get assistance."

This kind of positive reception really bears on the program sustainability issue. If we want robust social policies we should look toward universalistic programs that take the question of the moral quality of the poor off the table.

Redefining work as a measure of our identity and productivity in the world

March 18, 2016

Roderick Benns recently interviewed Michael Vertolli, a PhD student at Carleton University who studies artificial intelligence in relation to human cognition. He believes that basic income is one of the only ways to move forward in a future of large-scale automation.

Benns: *What is the connection between automation and basic income? Why should we be considering this social policy change based on automation trends — hasn't this always been predicted and yet we still seem to have jobs?*

Vertolli: The short answer is that the belief that "we still seem to have jobs" is a misleading perception held by people whose jobs have yet to get significantly affected. This means it is held by people in the middle-class range with medium-difficulty jobs that require one to think. The problem is systems like AlphaGo, Google's Artificial Intelligence that just beat the world champion at Go, demonstrate that even these tasks can now be learned by sufficiently powerful AIs.

To put it even more bluntly, I could probably replace most of the staff in the head office of most companies with a single tech or small team. And, I could do that using simple automation in most cases. More complex cases require more complex techniques, but we now have those. This would have a significant initial cost, and I expect that is one of the major contemporary deterrents. However, companies like Google and McDonald's don't have this problem and they set market trends.

Unless everyone except highly specialized experts and CEOs (and most CEOs are probably replaceable with automation) wants to be unemployed, they best start thinking of solutions as soon as possible. Basic income is one obvious option that already has evidence in its favour.

Benns: *Should we be thinking about the nature of work differently, in the context of basic income? In what way?*

Vertolli: I think there are three major reasons why people work and each of them contribute differently to what work means. The first and most obvious one is to meet basic needs, such as food and shelter. The second major reason is for what I would call quality of life. This includes the purchasing of anything non-essential, such as a new smart-phone. Third, and finally, work is something that occupies people's time. If the meaning of work is going to evolve, I expect it will evolve along one of these lines or at least based on one of them.

To be honest, I think few people in modern Euro-American nations have had to deal with the first reason for a while. A minimum wage job can provide for a single person who lives simply easily enough. I should know. I have been a university student for nine years. And, with increasing automation, I hope that this will generalize to other nations that have been impoverished by our success more often than not. Thus, this reason is not really a good candidate for how we think of work.

The second major reason is probably one of the biggest things today and thereby motivates much of what the average, modern Euro-American thinks of work. People like to have nice stuff, myself included. But, if automation takes off the way I expect it to, then the cost of everything is going to rapidly decline. Nice stuff will not have the value that it once did. This means we have at least a couple options to consider here. We can either abandon our current way of thinking in favour of something else or we can try to maintain it. One way we can do the latter is by creating pseudo-scarcity by controlling the rate of production. In other words, we can perpetuate a sense of scarcity in order to drive the economy.

I think this is the best indicator of a complete failure to enter the 21st century, but that is just my opinion. I also think it can't possibly hold. The tech industry was built on the backs of some of the most anarchistic minds in the world and they are the gate keepers of all that software.

The third reason is the way I think we should go. If we buy the whole nine to five thing, work eats eight hours of the average person's day and I expect it is actually much more. This time is tied both to our identity and our sense of accomplishment, which is why there are such negative consequences for people who are out of work for a long time, including the elderly. Thus, the question is, in a world where no one needs to work for necessities or quality of life, how do we occupy ourselves and reward those who benefit society?

Or, we should redefine work as a measure of our identity and productivity in the world — not as a means to an end, but as an end in itself. As a fully funded PhD student, I live by this model and it is infinitely more fulfilling in my mind than what most people call 'work.'

Benns: *What do you think people most fear about basic income? Why or why not is this unfounded?*

Vertolli: Those of older predilections and times probably still hear communism in it, despite the fact that no contemporary forms of communism have a basic income to my knowledge. I'm not really interested in addressing this issue but it's there.

Another major reason is that the Boomers worked hard for their money. They are the second kind of work, in that they define themselves through and by that model of work. I can see almost every one of them saying, "You haven't proven yourself. You don't deserve nice things." But, that's just not true anymore: automation makes this metric moot. The problem is that when you challenge the model you are simultaneously challenging the Boomers' identities, and they are the ones with all the power, for now.

Those who don't fall into either of the previous two views probably are more sensitive to the social implications and required infrastructure change of such a move. For example, what happens to welfare and every other social service? What about the social stigma of living off of basic income or having it when others do not in the early stages? Basic income combined with automation will have as great an impact in the 21st century as both world wars did in the 20th. This is and should be terrifying. But, it's a good kind of pain with an incredibly improved quality of living for all as an outcome.

Moving to an entrepreneurial society with basic income improves capitalism

March 21, 2016

Roderick Benns recently interviewed Michael Schmidt, a Canadian entrepreneur, chemist and engineer. He was previously the founder and CEO of Listn, a mobile music start-up based in Los Angeles California before its multimillion dollar acquisition by Robert Sillerman's SFX Entertainment. He is now the CEO of Dovetale.com, a partner at PurifAid, a board member of K-Swiss and a member of the Canadian Leadership Committee for the G20.

Benns: *From your perspective as an entrepreneur, why is the concept of a basic income guarantee useful to society?*

Schmidt: Basic income is all about voice. Some people want more while some people want less. By guaranteeing everyone has the absolute minimum you can guarantee, as a nation that the basic needs of life are met. It's a win-win for the market and those who are in the market. It's a fundamental improvement on capitalism and even democracy, because everyone now has a minimum amount of voice.

As an entrepreneur basic income could come to reflect a new society. The people that want more can create more without as much risk. There will always be sizable risk when you're innovating. It wouldn't be called innovation if there wasn't. Here's the thing; people will always want to live their dreams. Basic income removes the minimum requirements to live. As a serial entrepreneur you're worried about so many things, but imagine if you have to worry about putting food on the table or paying your rent at the same time, I think these are distractions that inhibit some of the greatest creative minds.

Benns: *Do you see automation as a real threat to traditional jobs? If so – and more and more people end up having difficulty finding work — how can we still find a way to make a difference in society? What might still need doing?*

Schmidt: Of course, jobs that are less cognitively complex and more physically laborious are disappearing. That's a fact and they will continue to disappear. Just to be clear, I think it's a great thing. Automation makes us happier, we just need to make sure our economy catches up. Basic income is a step in the right direction because it allows society to become more creative. Some of society's best work is done in our free time and comprises the things we love to do, like contributing to Wikipedia or answering questions on Stack Overflow. Lots of disbelievers feel like society will become lazy with a universal basic income. I think the economy will become more efficient. If people are only given the bare minimum some will want more and some will be comfortable with just enough — and that's okay.

Enhanced capitalism, or capitalism 2.0 in my view, will be based on a more democratized economy. Things like the multiplier effect will have a monumental impact on a nation's bottom line. The Institute for Policy Studies reported that:

"Every extra dollar going into the pockets of low-wage workers, standard economic multiplier models tell us, adds about $1.21 to the national economy. Every extra dollar going into the pockets of a high-income American, by contrast, only adds about 39 cents to the GDP."

Fundamentally, this means that dispersion of wealth makes our economy stronger and laziness is not what we should be focused on.

Benns: *In the U.S., Robert Reich believes there should be a patent tax. He wonders if giving every citizen a share of the profits from all patents and trademarks that government protects for an extended time (say 20 years) might help fund a basic minimum income for* *everyone. They still benefit from the protection length of time and people benefit from this new way we could redistribute profits. As an entrepreneur, what are your thoughts on this?*

Schmidt: There are lots of creative ways to distribute wealth. This is one of the many ideas that seem promising or at least worth a shot, but at the end of the day we need to start experimenting. As a quick retort, I think companies should pay the people instead of politicians to keep things out of the public domain. That just seems like the right thing to do. While I don't think this is the only solution it's definitely a potential source for a resource-based wealth fund.

Benns: *What's the big picture take-away about basic income, in your mind?*

Schmidt: My perspective is simple. I believe that we are moving toward an entrepreneurial society as a whole. Big and small businesses flourish the best in neutral economic climates. I think things like basic income slightly de-risk starting a business for some people and can overall increase a nation's economic prosperity. This is mostly fueled by my optimism in the people. The strongest retort I've heard concerning basic income is that it promotes laziness. I think there will be people that abuse any system, but if the right stipend for the right locality can be found it can be beneficial on many levels.

I feel like as a nation Canada is extremely progressive. Areas like Waterloo, Toronto, Montreal and Vancouver have created innovation hubs and the next major innovation (as a society) is in public policy that increases a nation's 'happiness.' This is giving the people more so they can build more.

Small business would benefit under Basic Income Guarantee: Sylvain Henry

March 23, 2016

Roderick Benns recently interviewed Sylvain Henry, a trained biochemist, inventor, and recruiter who is trying to create new opportunities for the Canadian business community with his 10-week 'business trek.'

Benns: *Tell us a little about your business trek.*

Henry: Businesstrek is a 10-week bus trek across Canada to "blaze a trail for business tourism" that will boost the Canadian economy from the ground up. The primary goal of the trek is to discover, attract and create new opportunities for Canadian businesses and individuals, and then share this bounty online and during these travels.

The secondary goal is to develop a highly specialized crew of mobile recruiters and marketers who may then participate in future treks. This Businesstrek crew, a 'mobile economic task force' of 55 volunteer trekkers, will meet with businesses and business groups in boardrooms and coffee shops near the Trans-Canada highway. They will achieve their mission by using 55 smart phones and a simple, proven tactic. The bus will also be a 'classroom on wheels' where task force members will train each other, discuss new solutions, and share success stories along the way using a wireless microphone in the bus. All progress will be logged daily and shared on the Businesstrek.ca blog page via on-board Wi-Fi. This idea is barely two weeks old and it has already attracted sponsors and some crew members for its maiden voyage.

In addition to finding opportunities and developing new business relationships, the trek will also promote promising new ideas that could help stimulate the Canadian economy for all, starting from the ground up. Universal Basic Income is one of those ideas that will be campaigned across Canada.

Benns: *Why should businesses be interested in supporting a basic income guarantee?*

Henry: Universal Basic Income (UBI), or a Basic Income Guarantee (BIG) is a sky-rocketing, worldwide trend in 2016 which you can verify in Google trends. This new public benefit would be a seamless pass-through system that would top-up a person's salary if their income falls below a particular level. The UBI movement in Europe is very strong. Currently it is most active in Sweden, Scotland, Switzerland, Netherlands, New Zealand, Finland and Canada, since citizens of those nations are engaging their governments in discussions on this idea.

Here in Canada pilot programs are currently being proposed by the Manitoba Green Party, the Saskatchewan NDP, The PEI Liberals, and the Ontario Liberals. The Ontario Liberals will be announcing the funding of a pilot project in the coming year. At the federal level, the Finance committee has also proposed a pilot in its pre-budget consultation report. One of the most vocal supporters of UBI here in Canada is the former Conservative senator, Hugh Segal. Economists from the right as well as from the left are seeing its merits. So clearly this idea has widespread support. A North American Conference on Basic Income is being held in Manitoba in May of 2016 (NABIG). It will be held at the University of Manitoba and it is open to the public.

This is an old idea, as old as the political writer Thomas Paine. Now, due to increasing unemployment and the rise of automated work it an idea whose time has definitely come. From governments' perspective this simplified and more accessible system could replace welfare while enhancing Employment Insurance. The system would reduce the intrusiveness and size of governments, which would be very popular and practical. More importantly this safety net has the potential of eradicating poverty within a nation and creating better incentives for workers by tearing down the dreaded "welfare wall" once and for all.

Small businesses would benefit quickly from such a new system. According to Dr. Bart Nooteboom, Research director at the Research Institute for Small and Medium-sized Business, Zoetermeer, Netherlands. UBI would be "an incentive for start-ups...an alternative for ineffective subsidies for small businesses...and a deterrent for unfair competition from the underground economy."

Other advantages for small businesses include:
- stabilizing seasonal work
- reducing employee turnover, and dread of Mondays
- improving employee retention and developing loyalty to local employers
- the new source of spending income would be a boon for local subsistence businesses
- providing better work outcomes from part-time employees who have guaranteed shelter and food

Benns: *What role can businesses play to pressure governments for a basic income guarantee?*

Henry: Small business support is vital to the success of the basic income guarantee pilot projects. If small business owners would take the initiative to reach out to those involved in the pilot projects then basic income guarantee can help fill the sails of the Canadian economy and move it forward. To help facilitate this employer-employee tie trekkers will be recording video-interviews of small business owners who support the idea. The video interviews will be shared along the trek online and "en route" via the social media and our website businesstrek.ca. In these interviews we'll be discussing new business opportunities as well as economic stabilizers, such as Universal Basic Income.

Should the trekkers eventually attract the attention of the mainstream media we'll be happy to invite them to record our discussions as well. Perhaps the local media might inspire locals in other cities to campaign for a guaranteed income pilot project in their own cities. It might also inspire some of their local businesses to meet with our team for a coffee chat. Though we'll be promoting this idea in many Canadian cities we'll focus our efforts in cities that are currently pressuring their provinces to launch provincial pilot projects, namely (Manitoba, Ontario, Saskatchewan, Quebec, PEI).

Benns: *How does this topic dovetail nicely with what you are advocating for across Canada?*

Henry: Universal Basic Income is a great economic stabilizer for the "common economy" of individuals and and small business owners. Both are tied, more so at the local level. Businesses want clients and continuity of service with ever-changing market conditions. Individuals want a stable and stress-reduced life where they can focus their energies on improving their work skills, not fighting for survival each day. In this trek we'll help employers find clients and we'll also help people find employers.

Since small businesses are the economic and employment engines of any nation, then perhaps a universal basic income is the "binding tie" between all citizens and small businesses. The new income may fill the sails of the ailing Canadian economy faster than any global trade agreements.

Sink or swim, MP's petition to study basic income marked by his own childhood

March 26, 2016

By Roderick Benns

As a youth growing up in Calgary, Robert-Falcon Ouellette remembers being inspired by the 1988 Olympics. Ouellette's parents struggled financially, and his father was in and out of the picture. But his mother managed enough money so he could enjoy swimming at the City pool where he took to the water "like a fish."

"I was there as much as possible – I just loved every minute of it," says Ouellette, who is now Member of Parliament for Winnipeg Centre.

"Until one day a coach spotted me and invited me to join the University of Calgary swim team."

The coach talked to both Ouellette and his mother, but the cost was a couple thousand dollars per year. He remembers the coach telling his mom that her son had great natural talent which should be developed. But the financial barrier was too severe for the family. In fact, even the visits to the City pool for leisure swimming soon stopped, also for financial reasons.

"That was a real dream of mine," says Ouellette. "I'm still marked by it."

Ouellette, who has gone hungry before as a youth and even spent one summer homeless, says he is sure there are many stories like this that have played out similarly across Canada, many much worse than his. Persistent poverty and lost opportunities are the kinds of things he suspects would dramatically be reduced if Canada had a basic income.

A basic income guarantee can take different forms but it is generally understood to ensure everyone an income that is sufficient to meet their basic needs, regardless of work status. The rookie MP is determined to have empirical evidence of how such a social policy change might benefit Canadian families, by establishing basic income pilot projects in the country.

His determination to have data undoubtedly comes from his depth of education. Ouellette is something of a Renaissance man, with degrees in music, education, and a PhD in anthropology. He also has 19 years under his belt with the Canadian Armed Forces, retiring from the Royal Canadian Navy with the rank of Petty Officer 2nd Class. Even now, he remains a part of the naval reserve.

The MP, who serves on the House of Commons' Finance committee, recently invited Professor Evelyn Forget to Ottawa to make a presentation because he wants his Party to consider testing the idea in a few regions across Canada, including rural, urban, and on a First Nations' reserve. Forget was the researcher who unearthed promising data from the well-known Mincome experiment, which ran from 1974 through 1978 and which helped establish a minimum income for about a third of the people who lived there.

Forget dug up the records from the period and found there were fewer emergency room visits and less recorded incidents of domestic abuse. As well, less people sought treatment for mental health issues and more high school students continued on to finish Grade 12 to graduate. When she appeared before the committee, Forget recommended a basic income of $18,000 per year. It would be paid, when necessary, by using the existing federal tax system. People could still earn money over and above this basic income but Forget recommends it be taxed back at a rate of 50 percent on each dollar earned over $18,000.

241

When he was running for a seat in the federal election, Ouellette met a woman in a working class neighbourhood of Winnipeg who had been a participant in the Mincome experiment. It was a story Ouellette found inspiring. The Mincome money she received allowed her to go back to school to finish her education while she raised her three sons. Today, two of her sons have their Masters degrees, with one working for the City of Winnipeg and the other for Manitoba Hydro. The third son owns his own business.

"Here's a single mom who was always just trying to get ahead. She now owns her own, small home and she helped her sons do well. That's the hope for basic income – that's why it deserves to be tested," says the MP.

To that end, Ouellette has sponsored an online petition to bring pressure to bear on his own government to support further study. He will likely have high level supporters in Ottawa. Jean-Yves Duclos, federal Minister of Families, Children and Social Development, stated to several media outlets that a guaranteed minimum income is a policy with merit for discussion. As well, Senator Art Eggleton, has just called on the federal government to launch a basic income pilot. Quebec has strongly signalled its interest in turning their existing income support tools in the direction of a basic income guarantee and Ontario recently announced it would fund a basic income pilot in an undisclosed location.

"We often hear poor people just make bad choices. Sometimes societies make those choices for us, though. If we have a society that supposedly believes in meritocracy without opportunity, then you don't have a society of merit you have one of privilege – and as a society we just might be losing out."

More education, better jobs would be result of a basic income says Alberta entrepreneur

April 18, 2016

Roderick Benns recently interviewed Zachary Beaudoin, an entrepreneur living in Edmonton Alberta. He works in technology and believes the current economic system is unfit to deal with the shocks that will be created by the coming technological advances.

Benns: *From your perspective as an entrepreneur, why is the concept of a basic income guarantee useful to society?*

Beaudoin: First I want to explain the benefit of a basic income guarantee that I perceive as a citizen. I believe that a society as a whole benefits from having economic abundance for all. People would spend more time on education, learning, and leisure, become more politically involved and even pursue more fulfilling employment opportunities. The result would be a healthy, engaged, and progressive society with less crime and less suffering.

From an entrepreneurial perspective it is a matter of economics. I'm head of a company that makes video games which requires a market of buyers that have both the disposable income to purchase my product and the time to play. In a system with high, and growing, wealth inequality people buy fewer video games because they either can't afford to buy as many as they would like or they work very long hours to make ends meet and don't have the time to play so many video games. You can substitute videos games with any other consumer product or service and you'll see the same problem. So the more disposable income and free time people have the better for almost any consumer business.

Benns: *Do you see automation as a real threat to traditional jobs? If so, how can we still find a way to make a difference in society?*

Beaudoin: Absolutely. Without diving into too many specifics it is not only automation in the sense that most people today are probably familiar with – a machine replacing a human in some repetitive task. The greatest challenge to our current economic model will come from AI capable of learning to do complex tasks and manage complex networks with a speed and precision that is impossible for any group of humans to match.

I'll use one example that is probably familiar to most people: the self-driving car that the world's most powerful tech companies are developing. Most people I speak to think that it just means you can go to a dealership and buy a car that drives itself. What will really happen is companies in the transport services sector like taxis, trucking, hauling will replace their human drivers with self-driving systems because the cost will be lower. This will force their competitors to do the same or perish and very quickly an entire industry sector of jobs will evaporate.

During the same half-century similar new AI technologies will see service industry jobs disappear in the same way and speed. Within this century we could be living in a world where half the work is done by machines. The unemployment rate would likely cause the collapse of our economic system as it exists today. We'll need a new system that detaches income from labour. I believe that a basic income guarantee is not the solution to this future problem but it would provide our government with a means of absorbing the shock and buying them enough time to solve the problem.

Benns: *What makes basic income about equality?*

Beaudoin: I don't think of it in terms of equality I see it as shared prosperity because everyone would benefit. I also believe that it will play a critical role in overcoming the economic shocks we'll see relatively soon and that it is our moral imperative to implement it.

MP Blaikie supports basic income 'idea' but says it's up for grabs on how to define it

May 3, 2016

By Roderick Benns

NDP Winnipeg MP Dan Blaikie says he is proud of his party's recent support of the principle of basic income and says now the work beings to actually define what this means.

Blaikie – considered to be one of the most promising new MPs in Parliament – says he has "long been interested in the idea."

He points out that the recent resolution in support of basic income at the party's Edmonton convention was to affirm the party's support for the concept, study it further, and to support a pilot project.

"I was first concerned to get my party on board, to take a bottom up approach," Blaikie tells *Leaders and Legacies*.

For the new MP, he says his support for the principle of basic income is driven by his strong belief in social and economic justice. He also wants to prevent more conservative-minded legislators from using it as an excuse to support the dismantling of the entire social safety net.

"I've long advocated for social and economic justice, and an important component of that is income," he says.

Blaikie says that right wing thinkers "sometimes try to approach this (basic income issue) with the idea we should diminish services and pull the rug out from people." But the NDP MP says we will still need things like mental health supports, addiction supports, and affordable housing.

Since the NDP has a strong history of social justice, Blaikie feels that "we should be in this debate" in order to help shape the idea.

"The issue of basic income is up for grabs about how to define it. I think the overall concept is what's important because we know that people who have less income are more likely to fall into cycles of poverty," he says.

Despite his support for basic income as a concept, Blaikie feels it would still be valuable to increase existing supports compared to the status quo, if basic income was deemed unaffordable. This could include topping up the Working Income Tax Benefit, Canada Pension Plan and Old Age Security, among other programs.

When challenged that topping up existing benefits would not address precarious work in all its forms, Blaikie noted that "serious" Employment Insurance reform could help offset this.

"This is a policy option. We certainly need to recognize the changing nature of work in Canadian society."

The MP says if the approach ends up being to slowly expand the existing ring of benefits out, "it's better than nothing."

He notes government revenue has been in decline for some time, from income tax to corporate tax rates. "The idea that sufficient money isn't out there (to fund basic income) is something I'm not convinced of."

North American basic income conference a chance to turn 'good idea' into reality, says key organizer

May 10, 2016

By Roderick Benns

One of the key organizers for the upcoming North American Basic Income Guarantee (NABIG) Congress, says it's time to go from discussing a "good idea" to figuring out how to make it a reality.

Dr. James Mulvale, Dean of the Faculty of Social Work at the University of Manitoba and a basic income scholar and advocate, says conference participants intend to go beyond discussing Basic Income as a somewhat vague understanding "to mapping out how to make it a reality through cooperation among various levels of governments and civil society organizations."

NABIG is in Winnipeg this year from May 12-15 at the University of Manitoba. It expects to draw scores of people from across Canada and the U.S. and some from overseas. The focus, though, is North America, where the Basic Income Canada Network (BICN) and the United States Basic Income Guarantee Network (USBIG) compare notes and come with ideas for basic income developments through speakers and break-out sessions.

Basic income is developing more swiftly in Canada along the political spectrum. There is a groundswell of support from mayors and municipalities. The Province of Ontario is committed to do a basic income pilot project in the coming year. Quebec is also looking how to change its existing income supports to a system that looks more like Basic Income. Even the federal government seems to be open to exploring the policy in conjunction with the provinces.

Also known as guaranteed minimum income, guaranteed annual income, or a negative income tax, basic income would replace various welfare programs by providing a base amount of income to all citizens, regardless of whether they work or meet a means test .

Mulvale says the NABIG congress for this year "will bring together people from Canada and the United States who are involved in changing the conversation on income security."

"The message of Basic Income activists is resonating with citizens in general – that the old models of income security" are falling away, he says.

Such concepts as the "male breadwinner" family, the "full employment" economy, and means-tested, demeaning income support programs "are no are longer working in the 21st century," says Mulvale.

The professor says one key theme of the NABIG congress will be how Basic Income approaches can contribute to empowerment of and reconciliation with the Indigenous peoples of "Turtle Island" – also known as North America.

Mulvale says this year's congress will carefully examine policy design questions and costing scenarios "to help move us towards Basic Income programs that can gain broad public support and traction with key political decision-makers."

In Canada, Mulvale notes the new federal government sees a positive role for itself in ensuring the collective welfare. In the United States, the professor says innovative policy approaches are also being considered and debated within an election year.

Liberals ready to shake up Canada's social policy with basic income guarantee

May 30, 2016

By Roderick Benns

The federal Liberals have voted to shake-up Canada's social policy by moving toward a "minimum guaranteed income" model.

At the party's national convention just held in Winnipeg, the resolution states the party will, in consultation with the provinces, "develop a poverty reduction strategy aimed at providing a minimum guaranteed income."

Reaction from the Basic Income Canada Network (BICN) was swift.

"This is a very exciting development, and one that will inform Minister (Jean-Yves) Duclos' mandate to pursue a poverty reduction strategy," says Robin Boadway, a retired economics professor and BICN member. "Importantly, the resolution recognizes that the federal government need not await the results of pilot projects to move ahead with a basic income program with the engagement of the provinces."

Alan Gummo, a retired planner and public policy researcher, as well as a BICN member, says he is "particularly pleased about the unequivocal nature of the resolution."

"It is unqualified and unconditional thereby giving clear direction to the design and development of a national program," he adds.

In the Liberal Party's rationale, it states:

"The ever growing gap between the wealthy and the poor in Canada will lead to social unrest, increased crime rates and violence. Research indicates that a guaranteed basic income can reduce this gap, and create social security while being cost neutral. Savings in health, justice, education and social welfare as well as the building of self-reliant, taxpaying citizens more than offset the investment."

The rationale then recaps the famous Canadian Mincome experiment from the 1970s to support its arguments. Mincome's purpose was to determine whether a guaranteed, unconditional annual income caused disincentive to work for the recipients, and how great such a disincentive would be.

As the Liberal Party's rationale states, a final report was never issued, but Dr. Evelyn Forget conducted an analysis of the program in 2009 which was published in 2011.

"Forget found that in the period that Mincome was administered, hospital visits dropped 8.5 percent, with fewer incidents of work-related injuries, and fewer emergency room visits from car accidents and domestic abuse. Additionally, the period saw a reduction in rates of psychiatric hospitalization, and in the number of mental illness-related consultations with health professionals."

Quebec is currently looking into a form of basic income and Ontario has committed to doing a pilot project beginning this year to study the effects of a minimum income. Prince Edward Island has also expressed strong interest.

Senator Art Eggleton has been relentlessly pushing this issue, as has his retired counterpart, retired Conservative Senator Hugh Segal. Mayors across Canada are also on board. In fact, no less than nine provincial and territorial capital leaders support basic income or at least pilot projects, with innumerable smaller city and town mayors across the nation declaring their support as well.

Canadians' health through Basic Income: A prize worth fighting for

May 30, 2016

By Roderick Benns

As a youth, Tommy Douglas was a championship boxer. His success in the ring is all the more remarkable considering that years earlier he had nearly lost his leg to amputation when an infection set in. As his many biographers point out, a travelling surgeon agreed to operate for free, as long as his parents consented to allow his medical students to watch. After several operations, he not only walked again, he thrived as an amateur boxer and then built his reputation as someone who fought for the underdog in the political arena as well.

Douglas never forgot his childhood experience and resolved that no one should have to pay for necessary medical care. His efforts are now celebrated within Canada's history, for not only did he establish Medicare, he also established democratic socialism within the country and its politics.

While universal public health care is now taken for granted in Canadian life, there's a new policy kid in town that aims for the same kind of social policy immortality – a basic income guarantee. A basic income guarantee ensures everyone an income that is sufficient to meet their basic needs, regardless of work status. The type most talked about in Canada is a negative income tax, where it would be universally available during times of financial need.

With research clearly showing that being poor affects a person's health more than lifestyle choices, having a regular assured income for anyone to access when needed would address what is clearly the most important social determinant of health of all – income and income distribution.

As Dennis Raphael and Juha Mikkonen write in *The Social Determinants of Health: The Canadian Facts*, in Canada "income determines the quality of other social determinants of health such as food security, housing, and other basic prerequisites of health."

The Push for Income for Better Health

The Canadian Senate suggests that health care accounts for at most 25 percent of health outcomes. In other words, we know that it is income and its distribution that truly matters when it comes to improving Canadian health outcomes.

That's why many health-related organizations in Canada have stepped forward to fight for a basic income guarantee. A few months ago, 194 physicians in Ontario signed a letter calling on the Province to support a basic income pilot program. Following that, members of the Canadian Medical Association passed a motion supporting the concept of a basic income guarantee for Canada.

It isn't just physical health that is expected to improve with a basic income. The Ontario Mental Health and Addictions Alliance has come down squarely in favour of the policy, too. In a statement the Alliance points out that a disproportionate number of people with mental illness live in poverty.

"Evidence suggests that compared to current social assistance programs, a basic income guarantee could dramatically improve standards of living and health outcomes – at less cost to taxpayers. It would be particularly beneficial for people with mental illness and/or addictions and their children," their report notes.

Health units across Ontario have not been silent on this issue, either. The Association of Local Public Health Agencies (alPHa) is a not-for-profit organization that provides leadership to the boards of health and public health units in the province. In their resolution in support of basic income, alPHa points out that 13.9 percent of the province's population live in low income, according to the 2011 National Household Survey after-tax low-income measure.

Core Values

Perhaps basic income was always meant to be universal, and always meant to be tied to the same ideas and principles that brought us universal health care.

In 1968, the very same year that universal public health care spread out across Canada, a Special Senate Committee on Poverty reached out to Canadians to address the challenge of pervasive poverty. Chaired by Senator David Croll and unflinchingly written, it declared even then that Canada was ready for a basic income guarantee:

"It is the Committee's recommendation that the Parliament of Canada enact legislation to provide a guaranteed minimum income for all Canadians with insufficient income. This includes the...unemployed, those whose incomes are too low because they work in seasonal occupations, and those who are victims of jobs where the pay is insufficient to provide for their basic needs."

In fact, one of the authors of the report, Michael Clague, told social purpose news site, *Leaders and Legacies*, that basic income should come to be seen as a core Canadian value, just like universal health.

"If it's understood that all Canadians, like we have with health care, are assured of core financial security if they get in trouble, it makes it more saleable."

Selling it is what advocates have been busy doing, especially within the last two years. Their efforts appear to be paying off.

In its recent budget the Government of Ontario has pledged to "work with communities, researchers and other stakeholders in 2016 to determine how best to design and implement a Basic Income pilot."

The budget also states that, "The pilot project will test whether a basic income would provide a more efficient way of delivering income support, strengthen the attachment to the labour force, and achieve savings in other areas, such as health care and housing supports."

In Quebec, François Blais, the minister of employment and social solidarity, has been asked by Premier Philippe Couillard to figure out how the province might turn their existing income support tools in the direction of a basic income guarantee. Blais is well positioned to do so, having written a well-received book called *Ending Poverty: A Basic Income for All Canadians*.

At the federal level, Jean-Yves Duclos, federal minister of families, children and social development, has stated that a guaranteed minimum income is a policy worthy of discussion.

Tommy Douglas once stepped into the ring on behalf of the people of Saskatchewan and eventually walked away with universal health care for all. Ultimately, it will be Prime Minister Justin Trudeau who will have to decide if he wants to deliver basic income and the resulting health benefits to all Canadians.

Perhaps it is meaningful that our current prime minister is also a boxer. With the rise of precarious work due to automation and globalization, an economy in need of reform, and persistent poverty, he may come to realize that basic income, and the health of Canadians, is a prize worth fighting for.

This article originally ran on thinkupstream.net

Getting the big things right within a Basic Income Guarantee

June 13, 2016

By Robin Boadway, Alan Gummo, and Roderick Benns

Andrew Coyne gets many things right about a basic income guarantee, in writing an analysis for the National Post recently.

He gets that a basic income would not replace social insurance programs like Employment Insurance and Canada Pension Plan. He also gets, albeit with undue pessimism, that the provinces need to be involved. He acknowledges that the level of the guaranteed annual income program proposed by the Macdonald Royal Commission was inadequate, and he implicitly accepts that a basic income of reasonable scope could be afforded by combining the appropriate basic benefit amount with a suitable rate of claw-back as incomes rise. He even observes that a basic income need not deter work incentives; on the contrary, it will be enhanced compared with existing welfare schemes.

Most importantly, Coyne recognizes that mechanisms already exist for providing basic income to selected groups, especially the elderly through the OAS/GIS and for families with children with the Child Tax Benefit. These can be built on for other segments of the population by combining the Working Income Tax Benefit, federal and provincial tax credits, and social assistance into a 'universal adult income guarantee.'

But, as Coyne says, the devils are in the details. One detail in his article that is troubling is the view that a basic income would take all cash and in-kind programs and rationalize them into one income-adjusted payment. Much of the purpose of basic income is to allow people to escape poverty. Forcing basic income recipients to purchase their own pharmaceuticals and to fend for themselves in finding affordable accommodation would be counter-productive.

Housing and drug programs are not 'stand alone,' unrelated programs. In fact they often intersect with each other and with other support programs such as disability support programs. Therefore they must be carefully considered in relation to a basic income program to ensure that individual needs are properly recognized.

By over-simplifying Coyne is able to edge housing and drug benefit programs toward market solutions and public choice options in situations in which market solutions are not in fact available and in which some individuals need help making good choices. This is the genesis of the need for public policy and programming.

Viewing basic income as simply a replacement for existing programs of support for the less well-off belies the fact that welfare recipients and many in low-income or precarious employment are well below accepted poverty lines. A suitable basic income must not only remove the stigmatizing shackles of existing income support programs with comparable income transfers, it must also provide adequate levels of support which the current programs fail miserably to do. And it must complement rather than replace at least some of these social programs.

The assumption that in-kind benefits can be converted into cash overlooks the fact that many of these benefit programs involve and depend on the knowledge, expertise and simple human kindness provided by the persons who work in the programs. This type of benefit cannot be monetized and should not be eliminated in exchange for a basic income.

Public policy should always be based on real people, not theoretical people. With this in mind we have some doubt that real people make life decisions based on such arcana as marginal tax rates. They may well make decisions based on the net amount of money they can put in their pocket, or their take-home pay, but we doubt many people could identify their marginal tax rate if asked.

Understanding the needs and motivations of real people underlies our insistence that a basic income should be adequate at whatever level adequacy might be determined. Any discussion of marginal tax rates needs to be marginalized in the basic income discussion.

Robin Boadway is an economist at Queen's University. Alan Gummo is a retired city and regional planner. Roderick Benns is the publisher of Leaders and Legacies. They all advocate for a minimum income guarantee through the Basic Income Canada Network.

Diversity of voices at Basic Income Congress was a sign of policy's growth, says BICN chair

June 16, 2016

By Roderick Benns

After attending Basic Income congresses both nationally and internationally for about a decade now, the chair of the Basic Income Canada Network (BICN) says the latest Winnipeg, Manitoba congress beats them all in at least one area – the diversity of people attending.

"In the 10 years I've been going I've never seen anything like this one," says Sheila Regehr of the recent North American Congress, where about 150 people attended to talk about Basic Income.

"In its diversity it was absolutely amazing. We had the voices of indigenous people included, health professionals, legal scholars, public servants, professionals representing racialized populations, faith-based perspectives, and people from the LGBTQ community," she says.

The BICN chair says even the gender dynamics were better balanced, compared to earlier congresses where male voices tended to predominate. All of this points to one irrefutable fact, she says, and that's "that the Basic Income movement is growing."

"It's really exciting where this is going – we're having intelligent and informed conversations and that's a great sign," she adds.

A basic income guarantee ensures everyone an income that is sufficient to meet their basic needs, regardless of work status. The type most talked about in Canada is a negative income tax model, where it would be universally available to everyone during periods of financial need.

Regehr was particularly struck by the depth of the indigenous dialogues that occurred, as participants debated how a basic income would fit not only into their ways of life, but also how it could fit through the different legalities governing people living on on reserves.

The BICN chair says that even among activists who attended, there were those who came from privileged backgrounds wanting to make a difference for society and activists living in low income situations who had a personal stake in where the policy thinking was headed.

Powerful Moment for the idea of Basic Income

One of the most powerful moments for the idea of a Basic Income Guarantee came from the Winnipeg Harvest presenters. Winnipeg Harvest is a non-profit, community based organization that is a food distribution and training centre. The organization collects and share surplus food with people. Its ultimate goal is to eliminate the need for food banks in our community.

The presenters spoke about a man who had been homeless and who developed mental health issues. Navigating the welfare bureaucracy system had not been an easy experience for him in his late 50s, says Regehr, but something wonderful happened when he turned 65 – he started receiving the Guaranteed Income Supplement (GIS) from the government, since he was now an official senior.

"It allowed him some dignity," says Regehr. "It was something he was entitled to, and was therefore without shame, unlike the welfare system. He became housed – it literally changed his life."

Another presenter, Jenna Van Draanen, analyzed social media statistics around issues like basic income. She noted that the basic income terminology is capturing attention with increasing strength and that the vast majority of that online dialogue is supportive of the idea.

However, Regehr says Van Draanen rightly pointed out that just shows we need even more healthy debate.

"We can't just have cheerleaders talking to cheerleaders," says Regehr, "because understanding varied perspectives and challenges helps design better policy."

Basic income continues to dominate recent social policy thinking. In its recent budget the Government of Ontario has pledged to "work with communities, researchers and other stakeholders in 2016 to determine how best to design and implement a basic income pilot."

In Quebec, François Blais, the minister of employment and social solidarity, has been asked by Premier Philippe Couillard to figure out how the province might turn their existing income support tools in the direction of a basic income guarantee.

At the federal level, Jean-Yves Duclos, federal minister of families, children and social development, has stated that a minimum income is a policy worthy of conversation, opening the door to probable federal involvement.

Basic income remains the best public service

July 22, 2016

By Robin Boadway and Roderick Benns

As basic income policy gets more press as a way to drastically reduce poverty, inevitably there will be those who seek to preserve the status quo approach. This has served us inadequately for many years and yet there are some believers who remain. These same believers often seek to create false policy choices, as Armine Yalnizyan has done in her recent offering to the Toronto Star, 'Basic income? How about basic services?'

Yalnizyan, unfortunately, offers nothing new. She dismisses basic income of the universal sort recently put to a referendum in Switzerland on the grounds of cost. Very few advocates, least of all Hugh Segal who is providing advice on design and implementation of a demonstration pilot in Ontario, are proposing such a system for Canada. She then argues that a basic income of $15,000 a year would make many low-income seniors and some low-income families with children worse off. This would be true if the $15,000 replaced all benefits currently obtained from Old Age Security and Guaranteed Income Supplement and the Canada Child Benefit.

However, such a problem is easily overcome with a thoughtful and progressive policy design. From that she suggests, with no justification that the focus of basic income should be solely on provincial welfare and disability recipients. She dismisses providing recipients of a basic income an amount of $15,000 per year (which would be not too much more than what welfare in 1993 would be worth today).

She argues that a worker, given the choice between a basic income of $15,000 and working 25 hours per week at minimum wage, would choose not to work. This presumes that the basic income would fall to zero for such a worker, which would not be the case for a program in which basic income is income-tested — like a negative income tax or a refundable tax credit system. There is every reason to think this is the model being pursued in Ontario, and it's the one most talked about across Canada.

At the federal level, Jean-Yves Duclos, federal minister of families, children and social development, has stated that a guaranteed minimum income is a policy worthy of discussion, opening the door to possible federal involvement. As well, at the party's national convention just held in Winnipeg, the resolution states the party will, in consultation with the provinces, "develop a poverty reduction strategy aimed at providing a minimum guaranteed income."

From a municipal level, no less than nine provincial and territorial capital leaders support basic income or at least pilot projects, with innumerable smaller city and town mayors across the nation declaring their support as well.

Yalnizyan also writes that to raise everyone to the poverty level would require at least $30 billion a year. This is about half of the value of all non-refundable tax credits that could contribute to financing basic income. She suggests that such a sum could be put to use enhancing public services, and that this would somehow benefit everyone and be easier to see in an era of low growth.

In other words, she implies that making more public services freely available reduces the need for income. In some sense it does, but free pharma care, dental care, post-secondary education, and community and recreational programming does not provide adequate food, clothing or shelter. If faced with an either-or choice, we would rather ensure that people can afford the necessities of life than be given free public services.

However, a basic income is not mutually exclusive with public services nor a substitute for them. This is a false policy choice. Those without enough money for adequate food surely cannot be expected to eat sidewalks, dine on their tuition costs, nor consume new recreation centres.

— *Robin Boadway is an economist at Queen's University and is the former editor of the Journal of Public Economics. Roderick Benns is the publisher of Leaders and Legacies, a social purpose news site helping to lead the basic income discussion in Canada.*

Ontario appoints basic income advocate Hugh Segal as special adviser

June 24, 2016

By Roderick Benns

Ontario has appointed the Honourable Hugh Segal to provide advice on the design and implementation of a Basic Income Pilot in Ontario, as announced in the 2016 provincial budget.

Basic income, or guaranteed annual income, is a payment to eligible families or individuals that ensures a minimum level of income. Ontario will design and implement a pilot program to test the growing view that a basic income could help deliver income support more efficiently, while improving health, employment and housing outcomes for Ontarians.

As Special Adviser on Basic Income, Segal will draw on his expertise in Canadian and international models of basic income and consult with thought leaders to help Ontario design a pilot.

Segal has spent over 40 years in pursuit of a basic income guarantee policy for Canadians. He was chief of staff to former Prime Minister Brian Mulroney in the 1990s and associate secretary of cabinet in Ontario in the 1980s. Segal will deliver a discussion paper to the province by the fall to help inform the design and implementation of the pilot, on a pro bono basis.

The discussion paper will include advice about potential criteria for selecting target populations and/or locations, delivery models and advice about how the province could evaluate the results of the Basic Income Pilot. Ontario will undertake further engagement with experts, communities and other stakeholders as it moves towards design and implementation.

Waterloo Region largest municipality in Ontario to support basic income resolution

June 30, 2016

By Roderick Benns

Waterloo Region in Ontario has become the largest municipality in Canada's largest province to support the movement toward establishing a Basic Income Guarantee in Canada.

The motion – which originated with Kingston City Council and was sent to all municipalities across Ontario – called for a national discussion on the issue, urging the provinces and federal government to work together to "consider, investigate, and develop a Basic Income Guarantee for all Canadians."

Momentum continues to build for this new shift in social policy, which would ultimately usher in the end of the welfare system and the beginning of a guaranteed income from the government that would keep people above the poverty line.

The policy would ensure everyone an income that is sufficient to meet their basic needs, regardless of work status through direct cash transfers using the income tax system. Essentially, a basic income would ensure that no Canadian would ever drop below the poverty line.

John Green, founder of Basic Income Waterloo Region, said it is "significant to have large, prosperous municipalities like Waterloo Region acknowledge that despite their successes, they still have too many people living in poverty."

Green says poverty has a negative effect on everyone's prosperity, since inequality is understood to be bad for economies overall.

"Passing this resolution shows that Waterloo Region recognizes the potential of Basic Income to increase the prosperity of the region by ensuring that everyone is able to participate, contribute and enjoy high quality of life and well-being," says Green.

The Waterloo resolution report noted 12.7 percent of people in the region subsist on low incomes. The region was listed as the sixth most food insecure health unit out of 36 in the province in a 2015 report created by Cancer Care Ontario.

In addition to the municipal level support, nine provincial and territorial capital leaders support basic income or at least pilot projects, with innumerable smaller city and town mayors across the nation declaring their support as well.

Ontario announced a Basic Income pilot project would begin in 2016. The Province recently appointed long-time Basic Income advocate and retired Senator Hugh Segal to provide advice on the design and implementation.

Green points out that Waterloo Region is known for being progressive and innovative and hopes this will help its chances of being considered as a possible test site when the Province announces the new pilot's location.

Basic Income as an equity issue in remote communities

July 24, 2016

By Roderick Benns

It might not be surprising to learn that in Tuktoyaktuk, a community of about 900 people on the edge of the Arctic Circle, life isn't easy.

About 79 percent of the people who live there are Inuit. In 2012, 21 percent of the population received support in the form of income assistance. A full 85 percent live in subsidized housing.

Known simply as 'Tuk' to the locals, for generations the village was only accessible by plane in the summer and ice road in the winter. (The village will finally be linked by a two-lane, all-season road by next year – an extension of the Dempster Highway to Inuvik south of Tuk.)

One of the most difficult things about life in remote areas of Canada are the day-to-day barriers local people face, such as transportation issues and dealing with government bureaucracy. For instance, *Northern News Services* reported just last week that a woman named Clara Bates had her income assistance payments cut off this spring for not having paperwork properly filled out. She is but one of a group of Tuktoyaktuk residents who faced the same issue, according to *Northern News*, and it may be months before it can be restored.

Western society is becoming increasingly formalized. There are copious amounts of paperwork obligations for virtually everything in which there is a transaction of goods or services.

A basic income guarantee would only require each person to file their income tax once a year. There would be no monitoring and ongoing forms to fill out for this money for basic needs. It would create significantly more freedom for people in their already busy lives and remove the stigma of welfare. To get ahead beyond the basics, people would work to top up their incomes without fear of massive claw-backs like we have with the current welfare system. If there is no work to be found, they will at least be taken care of and less likely to use the health care system nearly as much, as decades of research has clearly shown.

It takes a great deal of energy and understanding to be able to navigate 'the system.' It takes a great deal more to do so in a rural context, whether in Canada's Arctic territories or even in the vast northern areas of our provinces. In the case of Clara above, and for people like her, having to regularly applying for benefits or services that are needed for survival is becoming increasingly immoral.

As economist and basic income advocate Guy Standing writes, "We must realize that the growing structural inequality is socially unsustainable...We must change that if we are to produce a good society fit for the 21st century, in which all of us have a life of dignity, freedom and self-control."

Basic Income Canada Network urges support in House of Commons submission

August 9, 2016

By Roderick Benns

The Basic Income Canada Network (BICN) has recently made its submission to the House of Commons Finance Committee pre-budget consultations, urging creation of a basic income that would be universally available to Canadians in times of need.

BICN Chair Sheila Regehr writes in her executive summary that this is "an important time to build on basic income initiatives underway in Quebec and Ontario" and on recent federal initiatives to strengthen other forms of basic income. This includes the Guaranteed Income Supplement (GIS) for seniors and the Canada Child Benefit (CCB) aimed at families with children, both of which have proven effective in reducing poverty.

In her summary, Regehr points out that income security for working-age adults "is very weak, some of it is outright harmful, and the resulting stress, poverty, ill health and other costly problems undermine the wellbeing of Canada's society and economy."

"The labour market is not providing everyone enough to get by," with more precarious jobs with poor pay and few benefits or protections.

In her submission, Regehr notes that the Canada Child Benefit is an excellent example of a limited basic income because the money comes with no strings attached for families. There are some prevailing stereotypes about what happens when adults are simply given money, she writes, such as that "people won't work unless they are forced by rules or deprivation," that "taxing people's income makes them reduce their work effort," and that people in poverty "are more likely than those who are better off to make poor decisions."

Yet it is the reverse that happens, the BICN submission notes.

"...people do better when they can meet basic needs, control their money and make their own decisions. Nutrition and learning improve, stress, alcohol consumption and violence decrease, and people are better able to find and create economic opportunities."

The BICN submission also points to a basic income as a "kind of infrastructure for individuals and families." It would allow them to be healthier and more productive in many aspects of their lives, whether parenting and caring, learning and developing skills, managing an illness, weathering a setback, working for someone else or creating something new.

As well as contributing to community health, Regehr says that basic income "supports the innovation agenda by enabling individuals to develop their own creative and entrepreneurial ideas."

RECOMMENDATIONS

BICN urges the federal government in the 2017 Budget to:

1) Take immediate steps in the direction of a basic income for working-age adults using federal refundable tax credits and other means compatible with the model of benefits for seniors/children;
2) Undertake a thorough review and exploration of ways, in the context of fair and effective taxation as well as poverty reduction strategies, to fully realize a basic income for everyone;
3) Cooperate with and support basic income initiatives of other orders of government, including by fostering public dialogue, consultation, analysis and policy development as this is in the interest of all Canadians.

Having a secure income is the first, best remedy for both education and wellness

August 22, 2016

By Roderick Benns

Social justice thinker, R. W. Connell, once said that: "Statistically speaking, the best advice I would give to a poor child eager to get ahead in education is to choose richer parents."

Connell's advice goes beyond education, though. Income is the building block for not only education, but our very health and wellness. Income and its distribution is the most important of the social determinants of health.

Support for basic income can be found within local, provincial, and national public health organizations. The Canadian Public Health Association, for instance, is calling on the federal government to "take leadership in adopting a national strategy to provide all Canadians with a basic income guarantee."

Ontario and Alberta public health associations have also indicated their support. This includes individual health units from municipalities across Ontario that also want to see the realization of a basic income as a means to improve population health.

And the long-term, upstream savings from having a secure, basic income in place are considerable. As basic income advocate Rob Rainer has written, we are "bearing massive cost from poverty, inequality and economic insecurity."

He writes that Canadian spending on health care tops $200 billion a year and that 20 percent of this — or $40 billion plus — is due to what are called "health inequities between lower and higher income Canadians."

Rainer also points out that the cost of poverty—in health care, criminal justice, and lost productivity—has been estimated at 5.5 to 6.6 percent of Canada's Gross Domestic Product.

"Our GDP is now in the range of $1.5-$2.0 trillion a year, meaning that poverty costs in the range of $82-$132 billion per year. Thus it stands to reason that as poverty is reduced, potentially sharply by Basic Income, the savings are going to be substantial," Rainer writes.

From an education perspective, there are few better positioned than Dr. Avis Glaze to comment on the need for basic income policy to address poverty. Glaze has worked at all levels of the school system in Canada and was also Ontario's Chief Student Achievement Officer and the founding CEO of the Literacy and Numeracy Secretariat.

Glaze says if we want to ensure Canada is a tapestry of safe and healthy places to live, work and raise our children, "then we must address poverty in a systematic and intentional manner."

"A basic income would be essential if we want to close achievement gaps," says Glaze. "From an educational perspective, this seems to be one of the most intractable issues in education."

In Ontario, Hugh Segal has been tapped to deliver a discussion paper to the province by the fall to help inform the design and implementation of a basic income pilot. Just how the Province plans to evaluate the pilot is unknown at this time. However, looking at the implications and outcomes within education and population health will be crucial as we move this innovative policy idea from theory to reality.

Basic income is not an alternative to work, it makes work possible: Dr. Danielle Martin

September 7, 2016

By Roderick Benns

A family doctor says basic income policy represents an acknowledgment "of the right to live a decent life."

Dr. Danielle Martin, a family physician and Vice President Medical Affairs and Health System Solutions at Women's College Hospital in Toronto, says increasing social assistance amounts would not achieve that goal because of the punitive way the welfare system operates.

"Rather than loading all kinds of rules onto people about their eligibility and policing their behaviour," basic income allows for the living of a decent life that "decouples income support from complex eligibility rules."

In an interview with *Leaders and Legacies*, Martin says understanding why someone might 'deserve' a basic income is old thinking in a world that has drastically changed. Given that we're at a "very different point now in our history" with globalization drastically changing labour markets, Martin says these dynamics are forcing people into uncomfortable transitions.

This means we "need programs that support people to transition from jobs that have become outmoded as industries face disruption," says Martin. "I think we need to stop thinking about a basic income as an alternative to work, and start understanding it is what makes it possible to work for many of our friends and neighbours."

Martin says the Brookfield Institute estimates that more than 40 percent of the Canadian labour force is at risk in jobs where automation is becoming more prevalent, which is also a global reality. She says when we look back at the famous Mincome experiment, as well as other more recent experiments with basic income, "the notion that a basic income reduces the incentive to work has been largely disproved."

"It isn't anti-work," Martin says, "to suggest that Canadians should be able to meet basic needs and protect their health while they strive to do the best for themselves and their families."

Like other basic income advocates, Martin is interested in seeing how the much anticipated Ontario basic income pilot will be unveiled later this fall in Canada's largest province.

"We're starting out with some very thoughtful advice around how this pilot should be designed and effectively rolled out in the province, so I am optimistic," it could lead to a full-scale program, she says.

Martin notes there is a "real opportunity" to learn about how we can re-think not just social assistance, but low income supports.

"Around the world from Finland to Utrecht, we're seeing more countries launching pilots like these to test the effects of new guaranteed income models, so it's clear that the time is right to explore redesign."

She believes it will only lead to more lasting change if the pilot is structured well, though, which means "a lot is riding on it."

For instance, she says the public needs to be engaged and they need to understand the purpose of the pilot, and all rhetoric needs to be countered with evidence.

'Everyone has a story': An interview with Dr. Gary Bloch on basic income

September 14, 2016

By Roderick Benns

Benns: *We're set to introduce a pilot on basic income here in Ontario. Are you optimistic this multi-year project will lead to a full-fledged model for the province and a measurable increase in people's health?*

Bloch: I am cautiously optimistic. I think a pilot like this is a big investment, and wouldn't be undertaken if there weren't at least some intent to follow up on the findings longer term. I am definitely optimistic that the pilot will find improvements in health, along with other markers of social and personal wellbeing. I am concerned that any reasonable broader scale-up is likely to happen after the next provincial election, which could easily leave the pilot orphaned under a new government that doesn't feel invested in its outcomes. That said, there seems to be significant interest in Basic Income provincially, nationally, and internationally, and a pilot can only add fuel to the fire of interested politicians and advocates into the future. So at minimum this will help build the pressure.

Benns: *How do you counter the 'Protestant work ethic angle' that we face here in Canada (and the US) about whether or not someone really 'deserves' their basic income?*

Bloch: In my experience, having worked for over a decade as a family physician with some of the lowest income residents of Toronto, I have yet to meet those mythological beings who are happy to sit back and live comfortably on government assistance. Most people know that engaging in society, through employment and other means of social involvement, makes them happier and healthier. Those who have the most trouble finding and maintaining jobs often have very good reasons for doing so - caring for children or other family members, dealing with disabilities, histories of adverse life experiences, and more. Everyone has a story, and once we are willing to hear those stories, we quickly become disabused of the false stereotypes that underlie this misconception.

Benns: *There are many people who work to mitigate poverty that say why not just top up our existing programs properly, since that infrastructure is already in place. Is this good enough?*

Bloch: Canada is blessed, and cursed, with a dizzying, complex array of income support programs. A few people find an adequate social safety net in there, but far too many fall through the cracks or get lost in the rules and bureaucracy. I am involved with efforts in Ontario to improve the income security support structure in this province, and I am hopeful we will make some positive changes that will provide both a higher level of support, and a simpler system to navigate, but this will require a broad and sustained commitment by government to implementing these changes.

A basic income program may hold the potential to simplify and supersede at least some of the existing programs. That said, a basic income program could easily suffer from some of the same pitfalls as people face now, especially in providing an income that is inadequate to meet the needs of individuals and families. So, there may be other acceptable approaches to building a decent social safety net, but the idea of a basic income is attractive in that it could meet the goals of making income supports simple to access, portable, and (if it is structured appropriately) adequate to protect health and wellbeing; and it could do so without the stigmatizing and dehumanizing principles underlying our current system of social assistance.

Growing a movement: Basic income in the Canadian context

By Roderick Benns and Jenna Van Draanen

Every great movement springs from the unmet needs of the people. Every successful movement occurs when those same needs are recognised by a willing faction of innovative policy makers, not afraid to challenge the old ways.

Here, then, is the basic income movement in Canada, on the cusp of convergence of these two truths. On the one hand, a precarious class of people has risen, made up of lower income workers trapped in part-time work, millennials feeling a sense of career frustration and urgency, and educated professionals trapped in perennial cycles of contract work. The same story plays out in the UK, US, and other western nations. On the other hand, there is growing high level political support across all three levels of Canada's political system — municipal, provincial, and federal — to remedy this through some form of guaranteed minimum income.

A Health Imperative

Basic income manages to straddle a broad range of critical public policy, and none as important as population health.

There is strong evidence for the benefits of this social policy from the health sector, and especially from work that demonstrates the impact of the social determinants of health on population-level health outcomes. There is also strong support alongside this evidence from many health organizations and health practitioners in Canada. We know, for instance, that human health is shaped by a combination of genetic and biological factors, lifestyle factors, and social and environmental factors. Up to 50 percent of health outcomes are determined by key social factors including household income, housing, food, education, and early childhood development. In this way, guaranteeing a minimum income floor beneath which no one can fall can have a marked impact on the health of a population.

Data from the Wellesley Institute indicate that increasing the income of the poorest two deciles of Canadians by $1000 per year would result in 10,000 fewer diagnoses of chronic disease and 6,600 fewer disability days every two weeks — a dramatic improvement. Experts estimate that even just moving people from the lowest to the second lowest income bracket would save $7.6 billion in annual health expenditures and note that at least 20 percent of the $200 billion spent on health care annually is attributable to socio-economic disparities in Canada. Basic income presents a real solution to these challenges and a way to capitalize on these opportunities to improve Canadians' health, and health organizations are showing their support in droves.

Support for this policy can be found within local, provincial, and national public health organizations. The Canadian Public Health Association, a professional association of public health practitioners, is calling on the federal government to "take leadership in adopting a national strategy to provide all Canadians with a basic income guarantee."

The Alberta and Ontario Public Health Associations have made similar clear statements. A growing number of local health units from municipalities across Canada's largest province, Ontario, have endorsed the concept of a basic income including the Haliburton, Kawartha Pine Ridge, Simcoe Muskoka, and Sudbury District Health Units, for example. The health units agree that a guaranteed minimum income could give families living in poverty the ability to meet their basic needs. They note that a basic income guarantee could have "health promoting effects, and reduce health and social inequities. It is considered to have merits as an effective policy option."

Other public health organizations in Ontario are saying the same thing. In fact, the Association of Local Public Health Agencies and the Ontario Boards of Health (organizations which contain local public health units among their members) have also endorsed basic income and are calling on federal and provincial ministers to investigate basic income further. The official position of these groups is that they are requesting that the federal ministers across a broad range of government ministries prioritize "joint federal-consideration and investigation into a basic income guarantee as a policy option for reducing poverty and income insecurity."

Key medical associations in the country have come out in support of basic income as well. In 2015, 194 physicians in Ontario signed on to a letter in support of basic income that went to the Ontario Health Minister, Eric Hoskins. In addition, the Canadian Medical Association has publically voiced their support for a basic income.

Understanding Canadian Support

Why such strong support for basic income from these various health associations in Canada, and why now? Most of the organizations and individuals mentioned here have cited growing income inequality, the detrimental effects of low income on health, and the insufficiency of current income security programs as the impetus for this call to action. There is also positive evidence from the well-known Manitoba pilot in the 1970s, in Dauphin, and similar cash transfer programs for children and seniors that have improved health for those groups. The universality of the income guarantee are all listed as reasons why these groups are offering their support for basic income in particular.

In a move that excited basic income advocates, in its recent budget Ontario has pledged to "work with communities, researchers and other stakeholders in 2016 to determine how best to design and implement a Basic Income pilot."

In neighbouring Quebec, Canada's largest province by area and second largest in population, François Blais is the minister of employment and social solidarity. He was recently tasked with figuring out how the province might turn their existing income support tools in the direction of a basic income guarantee. Blais is well positioned to do so, having written a book on this topic called *Ending Poverty: A Basic Income for All Canadians*.

At the federal level where Canada's new Liberal Party has taken the country by storm in its embrace of progressive policies, Jean-Yves Duclos, the Minister of Families, Children and Social Development, has stated that a guaranteed minimum income is a policy worthy of discussion. This opens the door to possible federal involvement. As well, key senators like Liberal Art Eggleton has been relentlessly pushing this issue, as has his retired counterpart, Conservative Senator Hugh Segal, who was also brought in as adviser for the Ontario pilot.

In Canada's cities, the political support is significant. It includes big city mayors like Calgary's Mayor Naheed Nenshi, Edmonton's Mayor Don Iveson and Halifax's Mike Savage. In fact, no less than nine provincial and territorial capital leaders support basic income or at least pilot projects, with innumerable smaller city and town mayors across the nation declaring their support as well. They know — as government leaders who are closest to the people — that a guaranteed income would reduce inequities in their communities, reduce crime, improve health outcomes, and strengthen social cohesion.

At the Liberal Party's national convention recently held in Winnipeg, the resolution states the federal Liberals will, in consultation with the provinces, "develop a poverty reduction strategy aimed at providing a minimum guaranteed income."

In Sum

The man who founded Medicare in Canada, Tommy Douglas, nearly lost his leg to amputation when an infection set in. As his many biographers tell, a travelling surgeon agreed to operate for free, as long as his parents allowed his medical students to watch. After several operations, Douglas not only walked again, he never forgot his childhood experience. He resolved that no one should have to pay for necessary medical care. His efforts are now celebrated within Canada's history, for not only did he establish Medicare, he also established democratic socialism here.

That same democratic socialism is on the verge of a massive amplification, should basic income be adopted. As we know from Medicare's historical example, the policy began in Saskatchewan and was quickly adopted by the nation. If even one province in Canada makes this leap then more will follow.

Such a transformation would not end at Canada's borders. If a wealthy, G7 nation like Canada were to adopt some form of basic income policy, it would surely signal a social economy revolution for the world. With the unstoppable forces of globalization and automation, the pressure and insistence for change is palpable. We now have the willing policy makers. We have the unmet needs of the people, their voices clear.

Change is coming.

Roderick Benns is the publisher of Leaders and Legacies, a social purpose news site that has been a leading proponent of basic income policy. Jenna Van Draanen is a public health practitioner, researcher and evaluator dedicated to social justice and addressing the social determinants of health and well-being. This article was originally written for inclusion in **It's Basic Income**, *a compilation of essays on basic income policy.*

Basic income would help the most 'egregious forms of poverty,' says Raphael

By Roderick Benns

A basic income guarantee is not a magic bullet for all forms of economic deprivation in our society, according to a York University professor – but it's absolutely necessary for the most severe instances of poverty.

Dr. Dennis Raphael, a professor of Health Policy and Management at York University in Toronto, says the people in poverty within the bottom 10-15 percent "suffer profoundly."

"A basic income is a chance to remove the most egregious forms of poverty," he says.

Raphael has written over 300 scientific publications that focus on the health effects of income inequality and poverty, the quality of life of communities and individuals, and the impact of government decisions on Canadians' health and well-being. He is editor of the *Social Determinants of Health: Canadian Perspectives* (now in its 3rd edition).

The professor says as much as a basic income policy is needed in Canada, it cannot hope to do everything that is needed to address all poverty and health related challenges.

"For me to be really happy, there would also have to be housing supports, childcare, a national Pharmacare program, in addition to a better balance between labour and the corporate sector," says Raphael.

According to Poverty Free Ontario, in the last 35 years, except for a short period in the mid- 1980s to 1991, the poverty rate in Ontario has hovered between 9 percent to just over 12 percent, using the Ontario Government's official poverty measure (Low Income Measure – After Tax) and the latest Statistics Canada low income figures.

"Whether in good or bad economic times, since the recession of 1992, Ontario has struggled to stay below a double-digit poverty rate of 10 percent or higher. This tells us that reducing the poverty rate to 4 percent or lower will require structural approaches that address the basic material living conditions of low income Ontarians," according to the fact sheet.

"Poor people in Canada are really, really poor," says Raphael. "And Canada has among the highest incidents of low income workers – 27 percent of workers are low paid."

Over time, the poverty gap has narrowed for children and seniors, who are recipients of the Child Tax Benefit and Old Age Security, respectively. This fact has often bolstered basic income advocates' claims that a guaranteed minimum income could alleviate poverty for working age adults, too.

Since there are so many poor working opportunities, he says that a basic income can't possibly be a cure-all, when "insecurity and rotten work benefits" are still prevalent.

"There has been a relentless weakening of peoples' incomes," over the years, says the professor, and it's why he chooses to emphasize the need for a full spectrum of changes.

This includes better quality employment opportunities with benefits to create stronger income security for all Canadians.

A recent United Way and McMaster University study shows that fewer than half of workers in the Greater Toronto Area and Hamilton are in permanent, full-time jobs. Instead, about 52 per cent of workers are in temporary, contract, or part-time positions.

"A basic income is an absolute necessity, but it is only one small part. If the basic income could eliminate food banks, and if it can be in tandem with child care and Pharmacare, then there's no doubt this would be a profound achievement," says Raphael.

But by addressing a re-balancing of power between business and labour, such as the examples provided by Scandinavian and continental European countries, much more progress could be made, he points out.

"There are basic needs, and then there are the needs for a flourishing society."

Recognizing Social Inequities

By Roderick Benns

Social justice thinker R.W. Connell once said: "Statistically speaking, the best advice I would give to a poor child eager to get ahead in education is to choose richer parents."

Connell's advice goes beyond education, though. Income connects not only to education outcomes, but to our very health and wellness. That's why it was heartening to hear federal Health Minister Jane Philpott speak recently of "social inequity" as the greatest barrier to improving health for Canadians. In her recent remarks to the Canadian Medical Association, Philpott cited "social factors" as a key issue to be addressed to improve health.

This is the primary reason we must move forward with a basic income guarantee for Canadians. A basic income would be something that is universally available to all in times of need — no different than health care. We already have forms of basic income. This includes the Guaranteed Income Supplement (GIS) for seniors and the Canada Child Benefit (CCB) for families with children.

A basic income would cover the rest of Canadians who are currently left out and top up people's incomes to a set amount — say $18,000 per year — to stay above the poverty line. It should be an amount that is not enough for the 'good life,' but one that would replace a broken, ineffective and demoralizing welfare system that has been inadequate for too many years.

By collapsing the entire welfare system, these savings can be directed toward a basic income guarantee. Canadians spend more than $200 billion a year on health care and it is estimated that about 20 percent of this is due to "health inequities between lower and higher income Canadians," according to the Canadian Association of Retired Persons (CARP). The cost of poverty, touching on health care, criminal justice, and lost productivity, is estimated to reach 6.6 percent of Canada's gross domestic product. So there is substantial room for cost savings with some upstream thinking as well.

Those lucky enough to have good employment might be surprised to learn that the labour market is no longer sufficient to take care of people. Good jobs are in short supply. As a United Way and McMaster University study showed last year, more than 50 percent of all jobs in the Greater Toronto Area are precarious in some way, in that they are part time, temporary, or contract.

While low-income earners are hit the hardest, precarious work is rapidly creating economic uncertainty within the middle class, too. Even those who are highly educated are moving from one temporary opportunity to another, creating anxiety through an increasingly wider swath of Canadians. This is not a Toronto-only phenomenon. In fact, it is related to an economically globalized society and is affecting all Western nations.

The fact that the federal health minister is talking openly about social inequities is a great step. Now she must go further and champion a "health in all policies" approach. Every committee it strikes, every policy it examines, every decision the government makes should be seen through a population health lens. Supporting the creation of a basic income guarantee, in tandem with the provinces, would be a great first step.

The toleration of poverty is a continuing blight on our national legacy in a country where we should have a democratic right to equity. Canada has been blessed with a legacy of great leaders. It will be great leadership again — at national, provincial and community levels — that creates an equitable Canadian society for all.

— This column originally ran in the Waterloo Record.

Transformative steps are needed now to address poverty

By Roderick Benns

Waterloo Regional Police Chief Bryan Larkin is quite correct to lament the "worrisome" issue of poverty playing a significant role in the rise of shoplifting incidences in the region. As well, the Cambridge Times is right to suggest that "governments must do more to address the root causes of poverty."

It may not surprise anyone to learn that the root cause of poverty is a lack of income. However, there is a movement that has been gaining steam in Canada that could help change this. The idea is for the government to create a basic income guarantee so that no one would ever fall below the poverty line.

In some ways, it's incredibly simple. No man or woman in Canada would ever fall below a set amount that could be agreed upon to stay out of poverty. Let's say that amount is $18,000 per year. In other words, if you worked part-time while putting yourself through school and earned $12,000 a year, then a basic income would kick in with $6,000 at tax time. Or if you're a stay-at-home parent and only earn $5,000, then a basic income would ensure $13,000.

It would intrinsically recognize the value of work like raising children, caring for an elderly parent or the many other tasks most Canadians do every day without thought of monetary compensation.

As for paying for such a program, it would be imperative to dismantle the entire welfare system, boutique tax credits that help only segments of the population, and possibly the Employment Insurance (EI) program, too. These enormous bureaucracies could be made obsolete by a basic income. Such a new approach would be simpler, it would save money, and it would quite literally make us healthier.

We know that a lack of income is the single biggest indicator of poor health.

I interviewed retired senator Hugh Segal last year on this topic, considering he has been a crusader for such a program for 40 years. He pointed out to me that about 70 percent of people who live beneath the poverty line are indeed working, but they just don't earn enough. That speaks volumes about the quality of jobs that most Canadians have access to these days, a hodgepodge of part-time and contract work with no benefits. There is no doubt the trend is national, even global, among western nations.

A basic income would allow people a springboard as they are forced to take temporary and part-time work.

In the coming days, Segal will announce details about the Ontario government's pilot project on basic income. Researchers will study the effects of this policy over an unspecified number of years.

This could truly be a transformative step for our province and our country. In this most fortunate of nations we already have the money and the solution to eradicate poverty.

The only question we must ask ourselves is how we feel about the fact that we haven't yet chosen to do it.

— *This column originally ran in the Cambridge Times.*

About the Author

Roderick Benns is the publisher of *Leaders and Legacies*, a non-partisan, social purpose news site that takes a leadership angle for its progressive news stories, such as its series on Basic Income.

Roderick spent nine years as Senior Writer for the Ontario Ministry of Education's Student Achievement Division.

As an award-winning author and journalist, he has interviewed former Prime Ministers of Canada, Ministers, and Senators, and has written for *The Globe and Mail*, *Toronto Star*, and *National Post*. Roderick is a sought-after speaker on Canada's history and its Prime Ministers.

To book Roderick as a speaker about a Basic Income Guarantee or other topics contact him through **roderickbenns.net**

Spread the Word

If you are a basic income supporter, consider giving this book as a gift to someone you know. Blog about it. Or tell a friend or two.

The more people who learn about and consider a Basic Income as a viable social policy, the stronger the movement will become.

As well, if you are in **Canada** consider joining the Basic Income Canada Network (BICN), found at basicincomecanada.org. Regional networks are also listed here.

If you are in the **United States** you can join the U.S. Basic Income Network at usbig.net

If you are in **Europe or elsewhere** in the world check out the Basic Income Earth Network's *Get Involved* page at basicincome.org

Other Sites of Interest

scottsantens.com
One of the leading American voices for Basic Income

reddit.com/r/basicincome
An online basic income community

Made in the USA
Charleston, SC
29 October 2016